"Today's faith-based communities are being calle [...] story of how she answered this call is both pow[...] she sheds light and brings awareness to the realities of how children continue to suffer around the globe and how we can all help even the least of these, God's children in need. *Separated by the Border* is a book that will empower and inspire the reader."

John DeGarmo, director of The Foster Care Institute, author of *Faith and Foster Care*

"God commands his people to care for those vulnerable to injustice—particularly, immigrants and children. Gena Thomas and her family faithfully responded to these biblical injunctions by welcoming a five-year-old foster girl from Honduras into their home. In *Separated by the Border*, Gena weaves together her own story with the story of this precious girl and the brave mother from whom she was separated in the course of a perilous journey to the United States. In the process, she puts human faces on the complex but often politicized issues of immigration, asylum seekers, and foster care. *Separated by the Border* is a gripping, gracefully written story that the American church needs to hear."

Matthew Soerens, US director of church mobilization, World Relief, coauthor of *Welcoming the Stranger*

"In one powerful book Gena Thomas shares the trauma, hope, and love that is the migration of men, women, and children in today's world. Wrapped around her own experience as a foster parent, Thomas helps us understand why one flees their home country, even though they want to return. It is truly a remarkable book."

Ali Noorani, executive director of the National Immigration Forum, author of *There Goes the Neighborhood*

"Welcoming strangers is dangerous. All sorts of things might happen: it might radically alter your understanding of the world, change your politics, or your relationships. It will certainly affect your relationship with God. Gena Thomas's book is testament to the wonderfully transforming power of hospitality. I recommend her story to you as a daring and dangerous read."

Krish Kandiah, founding director of Home for Good, author of *God Is Stranger*

"When headlines and public policy debates filter down to the story of one mother, one child, and one US citizen willing to walk through the process, our focus changes from the macro to the micro. A story of grief, pain, politics, faith, endurance, laughter, separation, and reunification, this steps us out of the policy debate and into the individual experience. I wholeheartedly recommend Gena Thomas as a voice that has walked through real, sacrificial relationships using her Christian faith as a guide for each step of the process. If we want to understand how the policies and politics of the immigration debate impact real people, this is the place to start. This is a humanizing story that takes us beyond the talking points."

Alexandra Kuykendall, author of *Loving My Actual Neighbor*, cofounder of The Open Door Sisterhood

"Gena Thomas is a *maestra tejedor* (master weaver) who intertwines the tales of two courageous mothers with the threads of theology, history, and politics to produce a brilliant tapestry that skillfully exposes both the injustice of immigration and the wonder of restoration. Reader beware: this book will necessarily shatter your heart. Yet, it won't produce paralysis. Rather, *Separated by the Border* will grow your capacity to love beyond boundaries, borders, complexities, and documentation statuses. For the sake of our divided world, I commend this book with hope."

Jer Swigart, cofounder of the Global Immersion Project, coauthor of *Mending the Divides: Creative Love in a Conflicted World*

"In *Separated by the Border*, we witness the fierce, unwavering love of two mothers. In their eyes, we see glimpses of the heart for all of God's beloved children. Sobering and compelling, their story inspires us to step more fully into a life of dangerous and courageous love."

Peter Greer, president and chief executive officer of HOPE International

"In *Separated by the Border*, Gena Thomas skillfully weaves a story of heartbreak and hope in a world overflowing with cultural chaos. Yet this story is real, filled with helpful context and pointed commentary about little Julia and her family's lived experience. I found myself drawn in from the first chapter as Gena helped me understand and care about the complex terrain of family separation, asking me to follow her own brave soul into the place of being willing to do something about it. I pray this book makes it into the hands of those wrestling with their heads and hearts over immigration, deportation, separation, and reunification. Gena's words will help us rise and do what is right!"

Belinda Bauman, executive director of One Million Thumbprints, author of *Brave Souls*

"The immigrant experience in the United States is often seen from the perspective of depersonalizing statistics and dangerous caricatures. If we wish to make any progress in navigating through this massive conversation, we need real and compelling stories that expose us to the true and troubling realities many undergo, while offering a way forward. This is why I'm grateful for *Separated by the Border*. Gena Thomas tells a remarkable story and helps us see that hospitality is a powerfully subversive, prophetic act of God's grace."

Rich Villodas, lead pastor of New Life Fellowship, NYC

"I adore this book! It is a shattering read about the journey asylum seekers take to reach our border only to have their children taken from them. Thomas's book details the living hell Lupe, Julia, and Carlos experienced and how her family became part of the story. It rips out our stony hearts, giving us the opportunity to receive the fleshy heart of Jesus, the opportunity to receive grace. We endanger our souls and imperil the soul of our nation if we dare ignore this masterfully written account, the plight of immigrants, and our responsibility in all of it."

Marlena Graves, author of *A Beautiful Disaster*

"*Separated by the Border* is an essential book as our country has been failing at opportunities for compassion, morality, and wisdom on our southern border. Thomas illuminates the complexities and the human suffering. The stories she shares makes the issues deeply personal. Our hearts are broken—but we're also inspired by the incredible love in these pages that isn't restricted by borders. Like me, you'll likely be moved to tears, to hope, and to committing to help."

Kent Annan, director of humanitarian and disaster leadership at Wheaton College, author of *You Welcomed Me*

"The US has a mortifying history of separating families, dating back to the transatlantic slave trade. History reveals how racism and unjust laws have particularly decimated families of color—from Native American boarding schools, to mass incarceration, and our present immigration crisis—producing death, suffering, and trauma. While Thomas's book explains how this horrific narrative continues, it does so in a deeply redemptive way. Thomas tells a riveting story of personal transformation, detailing how God is using her family to bear witness to our Savior's love, mercy, and grace, in a time of fear. *Separated by the Border* will move you to tears, inspire you to learn, and empower you to act on behalf of the least of these."

Dominique DuBois Gilliard, author of *Rethinking Incarceration*

"*Separated by the Border* puts human faces to an issue that has been politicized, and it is gritty like the issue. At the same time, it shows the love, compassion, and caring of two mothers for a vulnerable child. I was so happy to see the story told in a way that helps people understand why we have this crisis and even more importantly that we are talking about real people, all created in the image of God. This is a must-read for all, especially people of faith, to see, understand, and have an idea of what Christ would want us to do."

Chris Palusky, president/CEO, Bethany Christian Services

"We need to look past the headlines to see how real people, real families, and real moms are impacted by and engaging with the policies at our border. Gena and Lupe graciously invite us into their story. Their choices are rarely clear or easy, but Gena and Lupe are always filled with love and hope. May this book inspire and equip us to enter into the stories happening at the US border."

Sarah Quezada, author of *Love Undocumented*, cofounder of Bridge Guatemala

"As I read *Separated by the Border*, I saw how faith, hope, and love were woven together to form an unbreakable bond amid unthinkable pain. This story challenged my naiveté as I read the horror that has ravaged lives at our border. You cannot read this account and then close your heart with indifference. My prayer is that this book will be a holy rouser to fellow believers who have cast a prejudiced and partisan eye toward our borders. Every person with ears to hear, eyes to see, hearts to feel, and hands to extend can support vulnerable families. Through this book, Gena gracefully shows us how."

Dorena Williamson, author of *ColorFull*, *ThoughtFull*, and *GraceFull*

"Gena Thomas guides us across various borders, helping us encounter and learn from a mother and daughter living the horrors and complexities of our immigration crisis. These insider accounts will move you emotionally and spiritually as you read this real-life story of two different families separated by borders but at the same time united by them. This beautifully written book gives voice to the many voiceless, nameless immigrants longing for a better life and risking everything for it. It's an important narrative that takes us beyond our news clips and political reads; these are lives forever changed by the dreams and horrors surrounding immigration in this country."

Natalia Kohn Rivera, special projects coordinator of InterVarsity's LaFe ministry and coauthor of *Hermanas*

"When women honor the stories of those whose stories may not otherwise be told, it unravels a song that is sung for centuries. Gena Thomas not only gives us facts about immigration and separation, but she honors story. *Separated by the Border* is critical because it is the story of a child who goes home, and it is the story of two mothers who are forever changed by a miracle. This is a story to be sung for many years to come. Blessed be the mothers."

Carolina Hinojosa-Cisneros, poet and writer, author of *Becoming Coztōtōtl*

"Gena's book is beautiful and godly. It's full of pain and inspiration. And sometimes, it's even hard to read (but for the right reasons). As a Latino, I am grateful this book exists. As an American citizen, I am grateful this book exists. As a follower of Jesus, I'm truly grateful this book exists! *Por favor*, read it, share it, and most of all, dare to be like Gena and her family . . . and live it."

Carlos A. Rodriguez, founder and director of The Happy Non-Profit, author of *Simply Sonship* and *Drop the Stones*

"Gena writes humbly and honestly about two mothers who find love and community through tragedy and sorrow. Her portrayal of an American family, an unaccompanied child, and a mother faced with hard choices humanizes the complex and real-life impacts of immigration. By writing about her experience as a foster parent to a separated child, Gena invites the reader into her home to see how our country's immigration policies deeply affect Americans as well as migrant families. Gena's generosity and honesty go straight to the heart and invite readers to reconsider immigration policy as a humanitarian issue and as a reflection of the values America holds dear."

Jennifer Podkul, senior director of policy and advocacy, Kids in Need of Defense (KIND)

FOREWORD BY
MICHELLE FERRIGNO WARREN

GENA THOMAS

SEPARATED
by the
BORDER

A BIRTH MOTHER,
A FOSTER MOTHER,
AND A MIGRANT
CHILD'S 3,000-MILE
JOURNEY

An imprint of InterVarsity Press
Downers Grove, Illinois

InterVarsity Press
P.O. Box 1400, Downers Grove, IL 60515-1426
ivpress.com
email@ivpress.com

InterVarsity Press® is the book-publishing division of InterVarsity Christian Fellowship/USA®, a movement of students and faculty active on campus at hundreds of universities, colleges, and schools of nursing in the United States of America, and a member movement of the International Fellowship of Evangelical Students. For information about local and regional activities, visit intervarsity.org.

Cover design and image composite: David Fassett
Interior design: Daniel van Loon
Images: hill houses illustration: © Charles Harker / Moment / Getty Images
central landscape of central Mexico: © Stocktrek Images / Getty Images
light blue watercolor: © andipantz / Getty Images
Mexican tile (186835054): © andipantz / Getty Images
Mexican tile (185224601) © ivanstar / E+ / Getty Images
Mexican tile (185228896): © ivanastar / E+ / Getty Image
girl profile: © Hill Street Studios / Digital Vision / Getty Images
old gray wall texture: © Vladimirovic / iStock / Getty Images Plus
blue water: © kentarcajuan / E+ / Getty Images
maps: © InterVarsity Press

ISBN 978-0-8308-4575-0 (print)
ISBN 978-0-8308-5790-6 (digital)

Printed in the United States of America ∞

Library of Congress Cataloging-in-Publication Data
A catalog record for this book is available from the Library of Congress.

P 22 21 20 19 18 17 16 15 14 13 12 11 10 9 8 7 6 5 4 3 2 1
Y 39 38 37 36 35 34 33 32 31 30 29 28 27 26 25 24 23 22 21 20 19

FOR LUPE

Guerrera de la luz. You expanded my capacity to see, feel, hear, smell, and taste the love of Christ as I watched you fight for and persevere in your love for Julia. Motherhood will never be the same because of you. I pray your story will harvest a garden of shalom. *Te quiero, hermana mía.*

FOR MY MOM, TINA

You are beautiful inside and out, and I'm grateful that your own story set me on a trajectory to meet Julia and Lupe. I know it hasn't been easy, but the fruit it has produced is uniquely amazing. I am confident Anna's legacy lives on in the generations that have followed her through you. I love you.

FOR KATRINA

You mothered in your teaching and modeled how teachers can be lifelong influences. Thank you for your love and faithfulness, and for constantly reminding me that we were all handpicked for this.

There is a daughter I mother,
A daughter I love—
But she is not mine and I am not hers,
Forever.
There is a mother she l o v e s
A mother who l o v e s her,
Forever.
For love is like water.
No human border   can   keep   it   out.
Yes, love is like water
It moves
above
in clouds
and
below
in
soil.
Yes, love is water.

CONTENTS

FOREWORD

MICHELLE FERRIGNO WARREN

In May 2018, stories of families being separated at the United States' southern border were beginning to make headlines because of the government's new "zero-tolerance policy" for asylum seekers. Online outrage was small but fierce. In true Twitter fashion, those of us working closely with congressional leaders and the administration, pushing for just responses to migrants, began to get tagged. Questions like, "How can this be happening?" and, "What can we do to make this stop?" were filling my Twitter feed.

Having worked alongside immigrants for years, I was caught off-guard that so many people were taking notice and wanting change. In reality, separating families is not new, so seeing people waking up to this injustice was very welcome.

My own immigration story is one of a young Italian couple heading to the United States via Ellis Island at the turn of the twentieth century to get jobs and send money back to their family, who had fewer opportunities to support those they loved. As for many immigrants, their goodbye was permanent. In recent decades, our country's immigration system has compounded the harm, indefinitely separating families through public policy in a myriad of ways.

Families around the world daily make hard choices for the best of those they love. They leave their families, moving for jobs to support aging parents and hungry children. They know that if they leave and succeed, none of them will be able to return home legally. America's economic engine needs more workers than our labor markets can fill, so we're quick to offer the undocumented opportunities—many in fields in which Americans don't want to work—so our lives can move forward without economic disruption.

US citizens don't realize the trauma and separation that befall those who pick our food, cut our lawns, staff our restaurants, clean our hotel rooms. This keeps our economy going, sustaining the age-old adage "We want your work; we just don't want you."

Economic pushes and pulls aren't the only driver of family separation. In 2014, thousands of children came to our borders fleeing violence. Gangs had killed their family members and recruited their friends, so their only option to stay alive was to head north as unaccompanied minors. These factors are still a primary driver for many in migrant caravans awaiting the opportunity to share their fears with US officials and be granted asylum.

Family separation is also an issue for children. Those born to undocumented parents often suffer the pain and trauma of having parents deported, not to mention of living under that threat. Over eight million US citizens live with that fear for at least one family member, and according to the American Immigration Council, "almost six million citizen children under the age of eighteen live with a parent or family member who is undocumented."[1]

Then there are undocumented immigrants who were brought to the United States as children: the Dreamers. They learned the Pledge of Allegiance, were educated in our schools, and contribute to our communities. They are in every way American, yet they lack the opportunity to move their legal status forward. Many Dreamers have a temporary protected status called Deferred Action for Childhood Arrivals (DACA). This status protects them from deportation, but DACA students continue to be used as political pawns in an ugly partisan game. So they wait for the opportunity to move from mere protection to the ability to earn legal status.

These examples make headlines in our news, yet most Americans, especially Christian Americans, seem to pay little attention. So in May 2018, when news broke about families who were coming to our borders, seeking asylum, and being separated, I assumed it would be just another day of tragic brokenness perpetuated and once again going unnoticed. But that was not the case. Multiple streams of response and outrage were expressed. And numerous groups lifted up stories, including the unique stories of Christian mothers.

The issue was finally making its way to the top of the noise. American mothers created photos of themselves and their children with #FamiliesBelongTogether and #NotWithoutMyChild and sent them to public officials via social media, calling for an end to family separation at the border.

On June 20, the backlash from the American people—most specifically the "church people," as referred to by the US attorney general—was so great the administration stopped the policy. Those who were new to the immigration policy game cheered and celebrated their collective success. Those of us who had been pushing back on the issues month after month were shocked. Something had worked. We saw that when enough voices with enough outrage and persistence say, "Enough," the madness can stop.

Voices were beginning to rise to the top on social media, and I repeatedly found myself drawn to the voice of Gena Thomas. Her posts were insightful and stirring. She had a unique voice that was unlike others, and I wanted to know a bit more of her story. I direct-messaged her on Twitter, and we talked on the phone. I learned how she had experienced the family separation policy as a foster mother and how she'd reunited that daughter, Julia, with her mother in Honduras. I was captivated by the way the Lord had carefully put Julia into Gena's arms to care for her and to get her back home. Such an articulate, deeply passionate, and gifted woman said yes to having a foster daughter and experienced firsthand what would become a global outrage: children being torn from their parent's arms for following asylum laws.

Around the time Gena and I had our first phone call, I was asked to lead a group of evangelical women to the Texas border. As I spoke with Gena, it took only a few minutes to know that I wanted her to come with us. She joined our group and visited the very places Julia had been. She walked through the facilities with chainlink cages and saw hundreds of asylum seekers sitting on concrete floors and wrapped in Mylar blankets, waiting to learn their fate. She met amazing faith leaders such as Sister Norma Pimentel of Catholic Charities working tirelessly to meet the physical needs of families seeking asylum. She talked with US Customs and Border Protection agents, whose humanity we needed to see in spite of our frustrations with the policies they were there to implement.

Our trip to these places had a huge impact on all of us, but Gena had a unique burden. While we all cried, her tears of lament and grief came from the most personal of spaces. When she spoke, it was from a deep conviction that comes only from walking alongside people in pain.

In its beautifully delicate yet prophetic calling out, this book stewards Gena's, Julia's, and Lupe's stories. Gena's ability to write with clear detail the brokenness of our country's immigration system can help us understand the issues that keep immigrants trapped and that keep families apart from opportunities to move forward. Her willingness to relive the pain and humanity of it all allows her readers to take in all that she has to share.

As you read *Separated by the Border*, remember that while migration is a global issue, and you may feel small in impacting it, this is our season to steward. Whether we have only a little awareness or a deep understanding, as Christians we cannot put our heads in the sand and hope the darkness will pass without our engagement. How we steward our time and resources matters. Unlike the foolish servant in Jesus' parable of the talents, we must not allow ignorance, fear, or being too caught up with our own lives to keep us from stewarding well.

We need to multiply what we've been given—our opportunities, our voices, our love, our homes, our families—on behalf of those who need it. Reading *Separated by the Border* and acting on what is learned is a compelling and practical way to begin to say yes to those who need it most.

INTRODUCTION

JULIA

How good is your Spanish? And would you be able to take in a four-year-old girl? She's from Honduras and speaks minimal English."

The social worker had texted on a Friday afternoon. I sat at my desk, bent over my cell phone, reading and rereading the text. My thoughts traveled to Honduras: *bachata*, *baleadas*, clothes hanging on the line. So many things in our lives seemed to have prepared us for this moment: our son was attending a bilingual school, I'm a former ESL teacher, and my husband, Andrew, and I speak Spanish, plus Honduras already had a piece of my heart. As those thoughts came, I tried to push them away.

The voice of logic came in loud and strong. We had just gotten into a routine with Emma, our foster daughter. Two foster children and two biological children would be too much for us to handle. Our first month as foster parents taught us this, and for the sake of everyone involved we knew it would be unfair to try that again.

A little later, the social worker called and left me a message, saying, "It looks like the Office of Refugee Resettlement [ORR] and Immigration and Customs Enforcement [ICE] will get her on Monday at court. It'll only be the weekend. Call me back after you talk to Andrew."

"We can manage four kids for one weekend. Right, Andrew?" I asked when he got home. He said he doubted it would last only a weekend, but I convinced him that if ORR and ICE were involved, they would get her on Monday. A few minutes later, I called our social worker back and said we'd do it.

When I walked into the social worker's office, Julia was sitting there in a brand-new, bright-pink Barbie T-shirt. The social worker said they'd found the T-shirt in their clothing closet, and Julia wanted it. Beautiful, soft onyx curls framed the girl's umber face. Her dark complexion made me speculate she was from a coastal region. She stood in dirty flip-flops next to the social worker's chair, chitchatting away in Spanish without a care in the world. "Julia's been talking my ear off," the social worker said. "She's so sweet. But I have no idea what she's saying." Another worker brought in a black tote bag with a few other items from the clothing closet, including a pair of sequined high-top sneakers that Julia had picked out.

I began to speak to Julia (pronounced *hooleeuh*) in Spanish. She seemed happy to hear her mother tongue, but her body didn't budge. I read that signal loud and clear, so I kept my distance and sat down on the floor.

"*Cómo te llamas?*" ("What's your name?"), I asked.

"Julia."

"*Cuántos años tienes?*" ("How old are you?")

"*Cuatro.*"

She looked older than four to me. I had been told her parents were deported, and she was left behind. She was under federal jurisdiction. I would find out later this was all misinformation.

I signed some papers and said, "We'll see you all on Monday."

I asked Julia if she would come stay with me and my family for the weekend. She smiled. I told her I had three other kids. Her eyes expanded with excitement. On the drive home, she jolted my Spanish from its slumber. The social worker wasn't kidding about how much this little one talked.

NATIONAL IMMIGRATION AND THIS STORY

On April 6, 2018, US Attorney General Jeff Sessions announced a new zero-tolerance policy in which the Department of Homeland Security and the Department of Justice would partner for the sake of prosecuting illegal entry into the United States. Sessions stated, "If you cross this border unlawfully, then we will prosecute you. It's that simple. If you smuggle illegal aliens across our border, then we will prosecute you. If you are smuggling a child, then we will prosecute you and that child will be separated from you as required by law. If you don't like that, then don't smuggle children over our border."[1]

Six weeks later, almost two thousand[2] children had been separated from their parents at the border since the zero-tolerance policy took effect.[3] When Sessions announced the administration's new policy, I couldn't comprehend the cruelty. I also wondered if it explained why a preschooler was living under my roof.

Julia had come to live with me and my family in February 2018, and it felt surreal to be a part of her story. She had first been separated from her mother, Guadalupe (called by her nickname, Lupe, through the rest of this book), by smugglers who were paid to bring them across the border. Julia had then been separated from her stepfather, Carlos, by US Customs and Border Protection, likely because what was recognized by the Honduran government as *stepfather* was not recognized by the US government as the same—a detail I didn't understand until an immigration expert read the first draft of this book and explained it.

Julia had already suffered much trauma and separating her from her stepfather had only inflicted more. The weight of the trauma we, as a nation, began inflicting on vulnerable children and their parents was cruel and unusual punishment.

When I heard that my own country was going to begin separating children regularly from their parents as a policy, it broke me. Reality became surreal, and Andrew and I learned to live in it, separating the trauma from our emotions so we could survive.

As the veil of Oz is ever-lifting from my white evangelical American eyes, what I now see is simply heartbreaking: government-secured human rights are mostly for privileged white people.

Julia is not white. Julia is undocumented. Julia's first language is
Spanish. Julia is a girl. These are all labels that set her back in a society
made by and for white, passport-holding, English-speaking males.

But God—who is neither white nor male, despite my use of the
pronoun *he*—shines his good news on every human being alive. The
good news of redemption is for every Afro-Latina. Every undocumented person. Every Spanish speaker, every girl, and every other
labeled person.

God does not show favoritism, and his arms are open to all (see
Acts 10; Romans 2). What I knew in my head this adventure taught
me to comprehend in my heart: God sees beauty in the places where
we've trained ourselves not to go. God sees beauty in the places we're
scared of, in the people we'd rather not talk to, in the middle of messes
we'd rather shy away from.

In 1 Samuel 16:7, God reminds the prophet not to focus on the
labels: "But the LORD said to Samuel, 'Do not look on his appearance
or on the height of his stature. . . . For the LORD sees not as man
sees: man looks on the outward appearance, but the LORD looks on
the heart.'"

Julia is beautiful to God. He formed her in her mother's womb, and
she is fearfully and wonderfully made. This book is a piece of Julia's
story: how she came to live with me and my family, and how she was
reunited with her mom, Lupe, in Honduras. This is also a piece of
Lupe's story: how she was separated from her daughter, and how she
was willing to return to the border if it meant the two would be reunited
faster. This is also my story: how God prepped me—and didn't prep
me—for this surreal adventure. These three stories are woven together.

You may find this story a bit confusing. Is it about foster care, or
immigration, or a five-year-old, or her Honduran mother trying to
care for her family? Or is it about a white American foster mother
finding herself? I had these same questions as I wrote this book. It
doesn't fall easily into one category. The way our stories intertwine

feels jagged and coarse at times, not like a beautiful braid of three strands that I wished it would be.

Our story is about two very different mothers from very different backgrounds and radically different identities, lives, and journeys—and those differences are sharp. Lupe and I look nothing alike. She comes up to my shoulder. Her long, wavy, dark hair frames her round, soft face. Her hard life has left scars on her plump body. She has been to the hospital several times since I've known her, because of all she suffered at the border.

I have short, brown hair with the right side of my head shaved. (Julia immediately told me this was not a woman's haircut!) I am five-foot-seven and about fifteen pounds overweight. When we met in person, I saw that, at four-foot-eight, Lupe had learned to command attention with her voice rather than her stature. Her beautiful smile could turn serious in a millisecond. She is a fighter who doesn't let others take advantage of her or her family. And she is a lover who showers hugs and kisses on all of her children regularly, and on Julia especially.

Despite our innumerable differences, we're both mothers fighting daily for our children to live in a better world. Ultimately this is a story of motherly love, which is one of the most powerful forces on this earth. So much of our past experiences make us the mothers we are, which is why I include a good portion of both of our backstories.

Lupe gave me permission to write this story. Some might wonder if her permission was coerced or that she felt obligated because of the power dynamic between us. It's true that our relationship will always be uneven because of the world we live in. But I didn't coerce her, and she has assured me she wants her story heard. She wants it to empower those who are deciding whether to stay in their home country or journey north. She wants her story to help people understand why many people from her country are trying to get to *el otro lado* (the other side).

Before I go further, I want to give a lot of credit to my local Department of Health and Human Services office. They were thrown a big loop with this case, and as complicated as it was, they ran with it and did everything they could to get all the paperwork for Julia's reunification with Lupe to happen as quickly as possible. I'm grateful for their around-the-clock work and flexibility, which helped them unearth the necessary solutions.

I imagine this story might pull at your heartstrings. But I want to be clear: I'm not telling it merely to evoke your emotion, your pity, or even your altruism. I tell you because I want my fellow Americans—especially my fellow white, middle-class Americans—to understand this is the reality of immigration. No, it isn't everyone's reality, but it is reality. For many women and children immigrating to the United States from the Northern Triangle (El Salvador, Honduras, and Guatemala), this story is not new or unique. It is common. Too common.

For those of us who call ourselves Christians, this normality should shake our faith. I am no theologian; neither am I an immigration expert; nor am I trying to speak on behalf of Central American immigrants. I'm simply telling the story I found myself caught up in from the whole of who I am. My reality crossed paths with Lupe's reality, and in it I found an amazing bond between a mother and her daughter. As detail after detail came to light, I continued to go back to my first encounter with Lupe, when she said she'd go to the border again if she could get her daughter back sooner. I had come face-to-face with relentless love in human form.

That love shook me. Lupe had risked going through hell a second time to be reunited with her daughter. This is the mother love of God.

While the stories in this book are true, some names and identifying information have been changed to protect the privacy of individuals. To the best of my ability and with the help of research, interviews, and tours of processing and detention centers in the United States, I have pieced Lupe and Julia's story together. There were some situations, especially in regard to dates and time frames, that Lupe didn't know, and asking her to think through the details would have added to her trauma.

I know that she left Honduras toward the end of October 2017 and returned mid-February 2018. The amount of time she spent as a captive is unclear. From research, it appears she was in a migration station—a detention facility in Mexico—about two weeks, though I can't verify that. My guess is that she was held captive by smugglers from mid-November through mid- to late January. She still suffers physically and emotionally from the abuse she underwent at their hands.

Some of this story is third person; other pieces are very present with my voice and my own theological analysis. The book is broken into sections labeled by country name. The story flows from Honduras to Mexico to the United States and then back to Honduras again.

MY FEARS

I have a few fears about writing this book.

The first is that I will do more harm to Lupe and Julia. I fully believe the truth will set us free, but I also know that most truths aren't transactional—especially traumatic ones. We can't just tell them and then freedom comes. I've tried my best to do as little harm as possible, which in some instances meant leaving details out of the story.

When I talked to Lupe about sharing her story, I was nervous. I had held off asking her a few weeks after the idea came, because I was scared and wrestling within myself. She immediately said yes. "You've taught me to be brave," she told me. The reverse is more true than words can explain as Lupe has embodied courage more than anyone I've ever known.

The second fear is that people will read this story, feel pity for Lupe and Julia, and then go about with their lives as if the story is an anomaly, as if the world doesn't actually work like this, as if this story isn't fruit from rotted systems. This is about a systemic issue, not an individual mishap. We white evangelicals must come to grips with the truth: salvation is not personal only but also communal. And many horrific experiences of nonwhites are systemic, not merely personal. When we work toward breaking down systemic injustice, we are also working toward communal salvation—not just the salvation of *those* people, but the wholeness—the shalom—of all of humanity.

Third, I fear for potential foster parents. I fear that I've laid out a situation you aren't willing to walk into. I want to be clear that this case was rare. I hope that if you are interested in fostering, this book will equip you, not turn you away. In 2016, according to a report of the Adoption and Foster Care Analysis and Reporting System, there were 437,465 children in foster care with 117,794 waiting to be adopted.

Yes, foster care is tough and complicated. Yes, it's hard to say goodbye. Yes, you need a support community to help you. But you can do this, or you can support others who are doing this. I hope that if you are a future foster parent, you will first admit your own daily need for a Savior and not feel as though you are a savior to a child. I also hope you'll find yourself deeply caring for the parents of the children in your care and will work to the best of your ability for the shalom of everyone involved.

Finally I fear that my white privilege may get in the way of this story. As a middle-class white American woman, I will never fully understand the difficulty of living in Lupe's shoes. But "proximity compels a response," says Michelle Warren in her book *The Power of Proximity*. "Its transformative lens turns what we see and begin to understand into action. The action may not even be something we consider a choice because we are so intimately connected with those affected. We share their pain and are compelled to do something with what we have."[4]

I didn't want the act of writing this book to be a reactive impulse that would end up causing more harm to a family I deeply care about. A lot of prayer went into this. Ultimately my hope in telling this story is for you to see the deep love of Christ through the love of this beautiful migrant mother. I hope it will conjure up the question, "How can we as Christians love our neighbors well, especially in such a divided America?"

Stories are powerful, and I pray the power that blooms from this story will equip others to see the truth and run hard after it, so that we all may one day, collectively and inclusively, find the freedom to flourish in true shalom-seeking, God-honoring community.

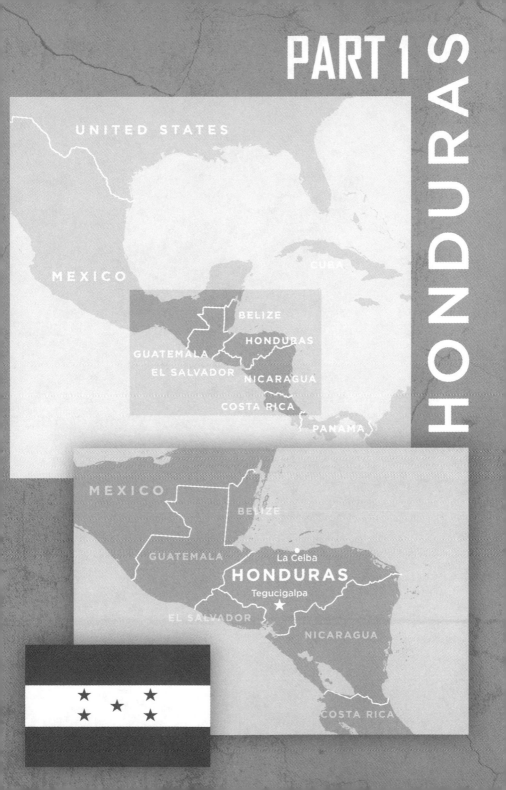

PART 1

HONDURAS

UNITED STATES

MEXICO

CUBA

BELIZE

HONDURAS

GUATEMALA

EL SALVADOR

NICARAGUA

COSTA RICA

PANAMA

MEXICO

BELIZE

GUATEMALA

La Ceiba

HONDURAS

Tegucigalpa

EL SALVADOR

NICARAGUA

COSTA RICA

Chapter One

EMIGRACIÓN

LUPE AND JULIA: 1996–2017

FROM ADOLESCENCE TO MOTHERHOOD

Lupe was born in a small town in Honduras in 1983, seven months before I was born in a small town in upstate New York. Not long after Lupe's birth, she was given to her paternal grandparents by her mother. Her mother moved to another city and rarely spoke to her. Her father, Pedro, was heavily involved in drugs.

"I'm going to teach you how to traffic drugs," Pedro told her when she was eight years old. "My friends will be your friends." By the time Lupe was thirteen, Pedro had been arrested and incarcerated. Lupe had to start providing for herself and her grandparents.

Lupe went searching for a good lawyer to try to get her father out of jail. She went to visit Pedro regularly, but after three months, he threatened her, saying, "If you don't get me out of here, I will kill a policeman."

She responded with her own threat: "Don't do this! If you do it, I will not come see you anymore. Or I will take my own life, and it'll be your fault!"

The next day, Lupe returned to bring Pedro lunch and found him looking for a way to fulfill his threat. He punched a policeman, and in retaliation, two policemen violently beat him up.

I can't defend him. I'm only a child, Lupe thought.

One of the policemen took that moment to demean her by saying, "The whole world will forget who you are." The weight of those words were palpable; the weight of her life was onerous. She could see nothing on the horizon that gave her hope.

Pedro was moved from the jail to a hospital just as a Category 3 hurricane came through Honduras. His life was nearly taken from him as Hurricane Lili killed five other Hondurans.[1]

Lupe, still thirteen, took her grandparents to a temporary shelter on a high hill. After she went to visit her dad in the hospital, she couldn't get to the hill where her grandparents were, because the wind was too strong. So Lupe went home alone.

One of Pedro's friends had become Lupe's "friend," and he knew she was alone. He entered her home and violently raped her. She screamed and screamed, but the wind, the lightning, and the rain drowned out her cries for help.

The next day, an older female neighbor came and helped Lupe clean up. The neighbor agreed to take lunch to Pedro in Lupe's stead. "Please," Lupe pleaded. "I don't want my father to see me like this." She never told her father what his friend had done.

The neighbor returned and told Lupe the news: Pedro was being moved to a high-security jail about two hours away. With little desire or energy, Lupe went to find a new lawyer. To free up some funds, she sold the house her family was living in. She and her grandparents lived on the streets for two months until she bought a small house from a friend.

Lupe went to see her father, hoping he'd be happy to see her and praise her for having enough money to be able to visit. But it didn't matter to him. "Buy more drugs so you can have a lot of money," he said. "And find a better lawyer." So she did.

The new lawyer told her it would take years for her father to get out of jail, and she began looking for other work to save money to get him out. But selling drugs was what she knew, and she had her grandparents to feed. At one of the parties where she sold drugs, she met a good businessman who wanted to know why she was drinking and selling drugs. She told him her story.

"Come work for me at my grocery store," he said. "You won't have to sell drugs anymore." No one had ever given her such a chance.

Years passed. At eighteen, Lupe fell in love with Jorge, a coworker at the grocery store. The two were happy and in love. She dedicated everything to the baby growing in her belly and to her loving boyfriend. It was a marvelous time in her life.

Before she told any of her family members that she was pregnant, the lawyer told her that her father would be released soon. She cried tears of joy but also tears of fear, because her father didn't know she was pregnant.

The day of Pedro's release, Lupe sent her grandmother to the jail to bring Pedro home. She stayed home to prepare food and welcome her extended family into the home for her father's return.

An hour before the party, Jorge arrived. "Where is Lupe?" he asked one of Lupe's aunts, who answered the door.

The aunt lied. "She left because she was scared of what her father would do."

Jorge left immediately and told his family. They sent him to the United States, scared of what Pedro would do to him. Lupe was heartbroken.

A few weeks after his release, Pedro said to Lupe, "Forgive me for having separated you and Jorge."

"Don't worry," Lupe replied. "I know that all my life I will suffer. You ruined my life."

One month after Pedro was released, his body was found riddled with gunshot wounds. He had died because of a drug deal gone wrong.

Lupe's dad was dead, and her unborn child's dad was thousands of miles away. Not knowing what else to do, she began selling drugs again. And she kept in contact with Jorge. When little Enrique was born, Lupe was full of joy. Not long after Enrique turned one, Jorge returned to Honduras and got involved in his son's life. But he and Lupe never married or lived together. He stayed with his mother, and Lupe rented a separate place.

Four years later, the two had another son together, Fernando. When Fernando was two, Lupe was pregnant again, with Samuel. Jorge always helped them out, but before Samuel was born, Jorge died from alcohol poisoning.

Lupe searched for better work opportunities as she had five mouths to feed beside her own: two grandparents and three children. She found work four hours away and moved there. Every fifteen days she sent money home to her grandparents and children. Every six months, she traveled home to visit.

Lupe then met Santos and started dating him. He helped her out a lot financially, and he was good to her. Three years later, she was pregnant with Julia. "I'm pregnant," she told Santos.

"You already have three boys," Santos said. "I think you should get an abortion."

Lupe cried all night, as she wasn't expecting such a response. She prayed, "God, you've given me three boys, and you know what Santos said to me. Please grant me this desire: let this be a girl. I will not abort her, and I won't abandon her."

"Leave and go home," responded a divine voice as clear as day. So Lupe returned home and months later gave birth to Julia—alone. She didn't add Santos's name to the birth certificate.

Not long after, Lupe's grandfather fell ill with prostate cancer and lost a lot of his memory. The doctor said he needed expensive medicine, and Lupe began draining her savings to pay for it. Soon she only had about eight hundred dollars left.

Her grandfather, who went in and out of being lucid, told her several times, "Daughter, I don't want to die." So Lupe felt pressure to find a way to help him. One day, her cousin came to her, and Lupe said, "I need to find a way to get my grandfather the medicine."

Her cousin replied, "I'm going to help you get to the United States so you can get a good job. But you have to bring your daughter to be able to pass through the border."

Though Lupe didn't want to live in the United States, she was desperate to get the medicine. This, she thought, was the only way to get it.

A SNAPSHOT OF HONDURAS

Honduras is a large Central American country with an area of about 112,000 square kilometers (about 43,243 square miles), a bit larger than the state of Tennessee. It was a Spanish colony until 1821. The official language is Spanish, and Amerindian dialects are also spoken.[2] The capital and largest city is Tegucigalpa, which is in the central southern area of the country. Further north is its second-largest city, San Pedro Sula.

Tourism often brings travelers to Roatán and Útila, Honduran islands off its Caribbean coast that offer world-class diving. The country also holds the Maya site of Copán, a UNESCO World Heritage Site that displays the history of the Mayan influence in Honduras.

Honduras's population of more than nine million has many inequalities, particularly in wealth distribution. Nearly half of the population lives below the poverty line.[3] In 2012, $3 billion came into Honduras through remittances, the majority from the United States.[4] This is an important factor, so as you read this book, keep this is mind:

> For many developing countries, remittances constitute a large source of foreign income relative to other financial flows. . . . Since remittances are largely personal transactions from migrants to their friends and families, they tend to be well targeted to the needs of their recipients. Their ability to reduce poverty and to promote human development is well documented and often reported as beneficial to overall development.[5]

Hondurans who have family members in the States often also have remittances coming to them regularly. Honduras's gross domestic product (GDP) is 13.8 percent agriculture, mostly bananas, coffee, citrus, corn, and African palm. Industry is 28.4 percent of GDP and services are 57.8 percent.[6]

Digging deeper into the GDP involves taking a closer look at the agricultural crops that make up such a large portion of Honduras's revenue. The banana industry has not only affected the country economically, it has had a spectrum of other influences over Honduran life that can't be separated from the current dependence on remittances.

The United Fruit Company was an American company that initially included Chiquita Banana, but in 1984 it became Chiquita Brands International and is now encompassed by Swiss-owned Chiquita Brands International Sàrl. For the sake of clarity, I'll refer to it here as United Fruit/Chiquita. It's also important to note that it was an American company until 2014, when it merged with two Brazilian companies.[7] It's one of the leading banana companies dominating the market and having had a hand in Honduran politics throughout history.

"If you think that the economy should serve the people of the country, then [United Fruit/Chiquita] has had a very negative impact [on Latin America]," wrote Adriana Gutierrez, professor at Harvard College, in an article published in the *Harvard Political Review* in 2017.[8] United Fruit/Chiquita has also been involved in political corruption within the Honduran government. During the 1950s, while the company worked hard to successfully overthrow Guatemalan president Jacobo Arbenz, it was busy in Honduras as well. "Encouraged by some social reforms, the Honduran labor movement confronted United Fruit in a process that peaked in 1954 with a strike that threatened the very existence of the Honduran government."[9]

Environmental destruction, including deforestation and the use of carcinogenic pesticides, was also part of the company's repertoire. Union activities were often suppressed, and in the 1990s United Fruit/Chiquita began a home-ownership program in Honduras and two other Central American countries that tied workers' jobs to their homes. When workers were fired, they lost their homes, so many stayed under the company's poor working conditions.[10]

A book review in the *New York Times* on Peter Chapman's *Bananas* sums it up well:

Throughout all of this, United Fruit defined the modern multinational corporation at its most effective—and, as it turned out, its most pernicious. At home, it cultivated clubby ties with those in power and helped pioneer the modern arts of public relations and marketing. (After a midcentury makeover by the "father of public relations," Edward Bernays, the company started pushing a cartoon character named Señorita Chiquita Banana.) Abroad, it coddled dictators while using a mix of paternalism and violence to control its workers. "As for repressive regimes, they were United Fruit's best friends, with coups d'état among its specialties," Chapman writes. "United Fruit had possibly launched more exercises in 'regime change' on the banana's behalf than had even been carried out in the name of oil."[11]

I include this information because it's easy for people like me to think that the Honduran economy is where it is because workers are lazy or picky about the jobs they do. Reading through the history of what multinational corporations—many of which are American— have done in the name of capitalism to the economies of Central and South American countries must make us recognize that our complicity in maintaining the American status quo has led to creating this immigration crisis. Economic colonialism is an effective and ongoing method of our current capitalistic economy.

Sometimes Americans say that immigrants are "invaders" trying to break into our homes and steal our jobs. "We must defend what is ours" seems like a justified response. But this perspective doesn't take into consideration that, in many ways, America has economically and politically firebombed homes and jobs, propelling people to seek refuge and safety at our borders. When we learn about the history and we hear stories of people involved, we start to see the complex reality beyond headlines and sound bites.

PREPPING TO LEAVE HER HOMETOWN

I want to make sure Julia will be taken care of if anything happens to me en route to the United States, Lupe thought. *I must find a man that can serve as her guardian.* Lupe already had a friend living in the United States: Marta. Marta's brother, Carlos, was also a friend. He was still in Honduras but was planning to go to the United States too.

"Carlos, will you consider traveling with me and Julia?" Lupe asked. "Will you consider becoming Julia's legal guardian? Think about it. It's important that she has protection."

Meanwhile Lupe worked on getting other arrangements set. She talked with Raquel, her aunt—her grandfather's daughter—about keeping him while she was gone. Raquel reluctantly agreed.

"He has to take pills every day," Lupe told her.

"I know."

"But he hates to take them," Lupe added. "He will fight against taking them. I had to be creative and put them in yogurt one day and a drink the next day. If I put them in the same food, he knows and won't eat it. He also does not like taking a bath. He will fight against bathing. But you must bathe him and make sure he takes his pills."

Will Raquel do what's necessary to keep my grandfather in good health? Lupe wondered. She would find out much later that Raquel stopped fighting him and therefore stopped giving him his pills. Her grandfather ended up hospitalized with a constant and caring visitor: Lupe's eldest son, Enrique.

Lupe had always been able to lean on her neighbor Anita and her family. These neighbors were more closely knit with Lupe's immediate family than with any extended family. Anita's husband had lived in the United States about a decade, but was currently back home. So Lupe asked, "Would you help take care of my boys while I'm gone?"

"Of course," Anita said. She knew and understood more than she wanted to: the desperation, the separation, the economic need.

Carlos also returned with an answer: "Yes, I will be Julia's legal guardian."

They began the paperwork, paid the lawyer's fees, and waited. Then they went to the Registro Civil Municipal to add Carlos's information to the blank spaces on Julia's birth certificate: ID number, last names, first name, and nationality of the father.

Carlos officially became Julia's stepdad—according to the Honduran government and according to Lupe—and Julia's name was changed to include his last name first. Her birth certificate now bore his name and a note dated October 2017: "A legal change happened."

GOING THE LONG WAY

Joining forces for the long route to the United States is not uncommon for Central American migrants. Lupe set out in the fall of 2017. In the spring of 2018, a similar group of traveling migrants made their way to the border. A journalist for Reuters interviewed a Central American builder about why he'd decided to stay with a caravan of traveling migrants in Mexico.

> Salvadoran Andres Rodriguez, 51, waited with a small backpack and a gallon of water in a field sprawling with men, women and children, mulling over a document that gave him twenty days to reach any border out of the country.
>
> Despite knowing the permit protected him, and that traveling alone would be faster, he feared if he left the caravan he would be exposed to the robbery and assault that befall many migrants on the long slog to the U.S. border.
>
> "It's much safer," he said. "Everyone is supporting us. One person alone is much more vulnerable. Much more dangerous."[12]

For women, rape is a true threat. According to an Amnesty International report, "Health professionals report that as many as six in ten migrant women and girls are raped on the journey. And activists repeatedly raise concerns that abducted women and girls are vulnerable to trafficking."[13]

The same caravan that Rodriguez was a part of peaked at a total of 1,500 but then decreased due to anti-immigrant protesting and resistance from President Trump himself announcing that the border

> was "getting more dangerous, 'caravans' coming," and as a result there would be "NO MORE DACA DEAL!" . . . "Republicans must go to Nuclear Option to pass tough [immigration] laws."
> A half-hour later, the president threatened NAFTA negotiations and wrote "NEED WALL!"[14]

More than 80 percent of the caravan was composed of Hondurans. Organizers said that many of the marchers were women and children who ranged in age from a month old into their seventies.[15]

President Trump's reputation toward immigrants preceded him. Lupe was aware of his consistent and negative words toward and about migrants. But she had no idea his policies were already reflecting his sentiments.

There are two other important factors that Lupe did not know. She knew the coyote would charge less to bring a child, but she didn't know this:

> Smugglers in Central America charge less than half the price if a minor is part of the cargo because less work is required of them. Unlike single adult migrants, who would need to be guided on a dangerous march through the deserts of Texas or Arizona, smugglers deliver families only to the U.S. border crossing and the waiting arms of U.S. immigration authorities. The smuggler does not have to enter the United States and risk arrest.[16]

Lupe also did not know that having Carlos's name on Julia's birth certificate would not automatically keep him and Julia together in the United States. If Border Patrol[17] used DNA tests to determine the relationship between Julia and Carlos and found they weren't related by blood, they could separate the two, assuming they were deterring child trafficking. And if Border Patrol required a marriage license between Carlos and Lupe to prove his stepdad status in the eyes of the US government, the two would be separated because they didn't have such documentation. Even if their paperwork passed, Border Patrol could still separate them, based on the timeframe of their arrival at the border.[18]

Chapter Two

EXPATRIATION

GENA: 2006–2007

E*xpat* (short for *expatriate*) is a label I've heard often among Westerners living outside their home country. Interestingly I've never heard Westerners call themselves *immigrants*. My own identity as the granddaughter of Italian immigrants who came through Ellis Island causes me to see the word *immigrant* as positive. As an immigrant living in Honduras and later in Mexico, I thought of myself as an expatriate, though the difference came upon me unconsciously. When I stayed in China with extended family who were living there, the word *immigrant* never crossed my mind. It was always *expatriate*. Kieran Nash of the BBC wrote,

> But what makes one person an expat and another a foreign worker or migrant? Often the former is used to describe educated, rich professionals working abroad, while those in less privileged positions—for example, a maid in the Gulf states or a construction worker in Asia—are deemed foreign workers or migrant workers. The classification matters, because such language can in some cases be used as a political tool or to dehumanize—as the debate around the word "migrant" suggests.[1]

These semantics bring to light that classism exists even within the labels we call ourselves. Most people agree that immigrants plan to live in a place permanently, while expats plan to live in a place temporarily. But if we agree on that as the only difference within the definitions, then if Lupe made it across the border, she'd be an expat, not an immigrant. And if I decided to live in Honduras the rest of my life, I think I'd still be called an expat by others, even if I called myself an immigrant. Let's be honest: expats are privileged in a way immigrants aren't. And for Americans like me who have lived in other countries, *expat* is our preferred label, despite an etymology that stems from "one who is banished."[2]

HONDURAS BY WAY OF ITALY FIRST

In reflecting back on my path to Honduras, I decided it was important to retrace my steps a few months before landing in San Pedro Sula, because the land we live on and the land we come from—if different— are equally important to understanding our identity.

I was born in Upstate New York to an Italian-American mother and an all-American father. When I was twelve, my family moved from a little town in rural New York to Michigan and then a few months later to North Carolina. I went to high school in a suburb of Charlotte, North Carolina. For my undergraduate years, I lived in High Point, a town about an hour and a half northeast of Charlotte.

After graduating in December 2005 with a degree in writing and minors in Spanish and political science from High Point University, I attempted to follow my career goal: get a job as a reporter in a border town. I applied and applied and applied to newspapers along the US-Mexico border and got a lot of silence or "thank you, but . . ." responses in return. It seemed my Spanish was far from where it needed to be for such a position, so I started looking for opportunities to live abroad where I could increase my Spanish fluency. Teaching English as a Foreign Language (TEFL) was the next-best thing, I thought. So I decided to pursue a certificate in that.

I grew up in the town of Corning in western New York. I lived in actual community with my extended Italian family on an almost-daily basis. Aniello's Pizzeria held my grandfather's name and many of my afternoons. Wiping down tables often landed me nickels and dimes from customers. These were spent at the most important store on Market Street: the candy shop. My cousins and siblings and I heard Italian spoken a lot, but we mostly just learned the cuss words for our own enjoyment. Saying them felt like we weren't actually cussing, and to this goody two-shoes, it was one of the few "bad" behaviors I allowed myself.

Growing up half-Italian also meant there was a lot of talk around our home and our extended family of visiting the motherland. The memories from those who had lived there were regularly served as consumables at my grandmother's succulent dinners.

At the ripe age of twenty-one, I had yet to see Futani—a small, mountainous town in the province of Salerno where half my heritage was housed, except for a photograph I'd passed a thousand times going up and down the stairs of my grandmother's house, which my grand-fathers built. I had a bit of money saved up, and I found a TEFL course in Rome, where my mother's cousin Zio Franco lived. Rome had enticed me, but Futani was the Italian lifeline into my heart. I had to see it.

Polinuro was a town about twenty minutes from Futani, right on the coast. My grandfather had a house there, and his lemon trees had been etched in my mind. I wanted to touch and smell and hear those places in person.

In January after college I went to live in New York with my grand-mother (actually my great-aunt) and grandfathers (grandfather and great-uncle), work at the pizzeria, and prep for my trip to Italy. I loved hearing stories of their lives in Italy and seeing black-and-white photos of them when they were my age. My grandmother would boast about her beautiful black locks of hair. "Don't ever get old, Gena," she'd tell me over and over again, looking up at her now-white hair. Her beauty had faded in her own eyes, but it hadn't in mine. I told her again and again her face belonged in a Dove commercial; she ritually washed with Dove and milk, and her face was always baby soft. She'd smile and pretend not to love the compliment. "You think?" she'd probe. "Absolutely, Meema," I'd reply.

One night at the supper table, I asked my grandmother, "Can you teach me some Italian?"

"*Mi passeresti il sale?*" she said to me in rapid-fire Italian.

"What?" I asked.

"*Mi passeresti il sale?*" she repeated, getting frustrated.

"I don't understand you," I said. "I can't learn if you don't teach me."

"Well, you better learn if you want to go live in Italy," she replied.

My grandfathers and I laughed, but I knew she wasn't joking. Her warning came from experience. She knew the hardship of being in an unknown culture with a different language. From her vantage point, language learning was survival.

The next day I returned to my "Learn Italian" books and tried to pick out words I recognized when the three of them talked.

Learning the language was proving harder than I wanted to admit. Nonetheless, in February of 2006, I set out alone for a six-week stay in the land of my ancestors. My immediate family decided they'd meet me there at the end of my trip. Finally my siblings and I would see the ground we grew from.

When I landed in Rome, Zio Franco picked me up in a tiny blue car. His daughters, who spoke English and whom I'd connected with to figure out the details of my trip, were nowhere to be seen. The airport was thirty minutes from his house, and he spoke to me in Italian the whole way home. *Did no one tell him I don't speak Italian?* I remember thinking. I have no idea what he said to me.

Franco's youngest daughter, Elisa, took me salsa dancing. I watched her and her friends move impressively to songs whose lyrics I understood. I'd thought of myself as a good dancer until I saw them. I attempted to dance too, although I'm still not sure that was the best idea. We drank really good wine and ate some of the best food I'd ever had.

Arianna, Elisa's older sister, took me shopping the next day. On a break from work, Elisa met us at the top of the Spanish Steps to walk around the city together.

The following day, I went with their mom, Zia María Rosario, on a school field trip with her preschool class. When we got home to their house, they had a cake for me, celebrating my twenty-second birthday. My TEFL class was starting soon, and before I knew it, I had to say goodbye to the beautiful family that had always been connected to me through blood but now was connected through first-person memories.

I began my TEFL class and figured out a time to take a trip to Futani. Zio Franco was worried because none of his family could go with me. I assured him I'd be okay.

Rome was beyond breathtaking, but Futani has stayed with me. My grandfather was one of five brothers. One of those brothers stayed in their hometown in Italy and ran a pizzeria there. When I arrived in Futani a few weeks after living in Rome, I embraced my great-uncle Marco, his wife, and their son. I happily ate at their pizzeria, and amazingly understood their Italian better than I had expected. Their dialect was more familiar to my ears than the one I'd heard in Rome.

They took me to the house my great-grandmother grew up in. We walked up one side of the stairs that jutted out from the curvy and busy cobblestone street, and we landed on the narrow platform that served as the entryway of the small concrete home. The arched doorway was all the aesthetic charm the home had to offer with its one room. It was empty and bleak if seen only with physical eyes but beautiful and charming when seen through the eyes of my soul. I had traveled all over the world and seen thousands of beautiful buildings, but this place, this small and simple home, held my world within it.

They say home is where your heart is, but in that moment, I knew the reverse was true as well: A piece of one's heart always belongs to the land connected to one's ancestors. That belonging is passed down from generation to generation, even when traditions and languages fade away. Seeds are born from soil, and they carry the essence of that soil with them forever.

I remember often looking at others in the piazzas or on the train, thinking, *Wow, I look like her. Wow, that guy looks like he could be my brother.* This may seem minor coming from a white American girl, but it wasn't to me.

A few years prior, when I was living in Nicaragua during college, one of the church leaders I was working with was sorely confused by my appearance. *"You're* American?" he asked for a second time with a bewildered look on his face.

"Yes," I responded.

"But what are you?" he pressed.

"Well, my mom is Italian, so I'm half Italian."

"Ohhh!" he responded with glee, as if I had just enlightened any and all his confusion.

The miraculous spirit of language cloaked me while I was in Futani. But I often tripped over my conversations with others in Rome. Spanish came out more often than I wished, much to the chagrin of my Roman neighbors. My goal was still to concentrate on improving my fluency in Spanish in order to get a job as a reporter.

Toward the end of my TEFL course in Italy, my classmates and I would go to the internet café and search for jobs together. Most of them were looking for opportunities in Italy or elsewhere in Europe. I set my sights on Central America, a place I knew and loved. When one of my English-only-speaking classmates announced she'd landed a job in Rome, I immediately thought she was brave to stay in a land whose language she didn't know. When I was honest with myself, I knew I was uncomfortable in Rome because of the language barrier.

I considered looking for a job in Spain, but as an American, it would be challenging to find a school that would work with me as an immigrant. I was told that I could get an EU visa because my grandfather was from Italy. The process would take a while and cost money. Also, the cost of living in Europe was significantly higher than in Central America, and I could likely get an automatic six-month visa in Honduras or Costa Rica as an American tourist. But I didn't have any extra money to live on while waiting for a work visa; I needed a job.

A few days before the rest of my family came to Rome, I found a job in Honduras teaching fifth grade at a bilingual school. They needed someone to start April 15, which was a few weeks away. The pay was decent, and housing was free. I applied and was accepted. The school year would finish at the end of June, which would give me three months to see if I liked living in Honduras.

My family and I ran around Rome then hopped trains to Florence and Venice. We drank cappuccinos and sangria and ate our fill of gelato, pizza, and pasta. We stayed in hostels until my parents couldn't handle it. My sister, brother, and I didn't complain when my mom booked us a hotel. Never before and not since have all five of us traveled to another country together. There was and always will be something special about the Italy that preceded us and the Italy we experienced together, even for my very American dad, who gave us one of the most American surnames on the planet: Smith.

Seeing the motherland was an utter privilege. In all of my other travels, I was told stories of people and structures and cultures that were fascinating yet far removed from me. But in Futani, standing in the house my great-grandmother lived in, I felt the pulse of my life-blood. Knowledge suddenly expanded as I saw a fuller picture of my people, their specific dialect of Italian, and their day-to-day lives. I had never felt the hunger to belong to a family, because I had always known my role in mine. But I'd felt the hunger to know where I came from more strongly with every story my grandparents told about Futani, like the weddings that the whole town attended, sitting at tables filled with food the family was expected to provide, set up in the piazza in front of the Catholic church.

That hunger had finally been at least partially satiated. More than a decade later, as a foster mom, I came to understand that the hunger I had is universal. This enlightenment was necessary for two reasons: first, for me to understand where my desire for adoption came from (also my Italian family) and, second, to correct my perception of the deep needs of foster/adoptive children. Not only is there a need to be part of a family, there is also a need to know where one came from.

TEACHING AND LIVING

Before I knew it, I was alone again, traveling to my next adventure. My flight touched down in US airports but flew directly from Italy to Honduras. I was happy to be moving to a land where I had a firm grasp of the language. But it took one day in the classroom to see that my grasp was weak in other areas. I was the worst at managing classroom behavior. The worst. But I could make the kids laugh, especially when I put my glasses on a dinosaur puppet to teach them science in a silly voice.

And I could make them cry—well, not actually cry but whine, because I beat them in soccer. That backfired some though. They knew I loved to play, so they'd ask me all the time if we could play soccer instead of having class. I probably gave in more than I should have.

I enjoyed teaching and really loved getting to know my students, but I had no formal training as a teacher. So I initially operated more like a fun camp counselor. Counselors deal with kids for one week. I arrived in April and had three months to finish out the end of the school year. I learned and learned and learned and taught a little and learned a lot more. They were gracious teachers.

I learned that Jonathan was really smart but struggled a lot with exams, so I tried to do one-on-one work with him when it was time for testing. I learned that Samuel drank a lot of Coke and did not need to. He was always full of energy, making the whole class laugh. I learned that Gricel was really anxious about school because her

English wasn't very good, and her previous teacher didn't speak any Spanish. We bonded well because when she didn't understand something in English, I would explain in Spanish. I worked on doing that less and less, and she understood English more and more. I learned that Crocs clogs are ugly and potentially an abomination for me to be wearing, according to the fashionistas in my classroom. I learned that unripe mangoes are tasty with a bit of salt on them. The boys climbed the tree across the street from school on our way back from PE so we could all partake in a mango snack.

And I learned that teaching wore me out.

My brain was so tired from being immersed in the culture and in trying to manage behaviors—often unsuccessfully—that when school let out at two, I walked eight blocks home and took a nap. Every day. When I woke up, I'd go for a run (always with a stone or a stick in my hand to repel stray dogs), come home, make supper, read, do some laundry on the washboard outside, write, sleep, and do it all again.

I loved living alone, and my small enclosed apartment complex was a great place for it. Across the courtyard lived my Italian neighbor, Gianni. He was about twenty years older than me. He didn't warm up to me much at first; but when he found out I was half Italian, I suddenly became like a daughter to him. He watched out for me and made sure I had everything I needed. He told me where the best place to get pizza in town was and introduced me to the best internet café.

One day he asked me how I was doing. I told him my stomach was hurting and had been for a while. He said, "Come, I will make you something to help your stomach feel better."

I was concerned. I had no idea what he was about to feed me, and I really didn't feel like eating. But I knew full well that "*Manga, manga*— eat, eat!" was more than a gentle command. There's a lot of culture— and potential offense—that sits behind those familiar Italian words.

Gianni sat me down at his beautiful wooden table in his small one-bedroom apartment, which mirrored mine. He sliced open a Mexican avocado (not to be confused with the bigger Honduran avocados) and placed it on a plate. Then he grabbed a one-gallon metal can of 100-percent virgin olive oil from the top of his cabinet. He lightly poured a bit over the avocado and sprinkled a dash of salt on top.

My stomach felt horrible, and I didn't like avocados. Every time I had eaten them in the States, they'd tasted rubbery. But I didn't tell him that. I knew if I didn't at least try, there'd be neighborly repercussions. So I reluctantly took a bite.

Are my taste buds deceiving me? This tastes wonderful!

I thanked Gianni and immediately felt better. He continued to watch over me, and I continued to eat avocados.

One day while at our favorite internet café, I suddenly fainted. Gianni grabbed my phone, called my mother, and began speaking to her in Italian. He arranged for me to be taken to the clinic and made sure I was well taken care of. Apparently I was dehydrated, and despite Gianni and my mom's plans for my parents to get on a plane and come get me, a few injections of electrolytes took care of it.

A LETTER TO MARÍA

The mother love of God that I saw so clearly in Lupe had been foreshadowed by another Honduran mother I knew, María. I was in my mid-twenties when I lived in Honduras, and María exemplified motherhood so beautifully I wanted to be like her.

Elí Romero, her son, was part of what we called the *mara*, a group of friends composed of several Hondurans and several American teachers.[3] He was a fellow writer and became one of my closest friends in Honduras. Later in life, when Julia came to live with me, Elí translated Honduran colloquialisms I had forgotten.

On our walks to the center of town and our camping trips with the *mara*, Elí often talked about his mother, María, and the influence she had on him. This resonated with me because she and I attended church regularly, spoke about God often, and had similar desires for the

generations to follow. While Elí had an understanding and appreci-
ation for the religious life, it wasn't his life—at least not yet.

María's spirited joy had been immediately evident when we met. A
few seconds into our first conversation at her home, she began talking
about God as if he was a close friend, and though I expected it, I
didn't expect to feel so connected to her so quickly because of it.
When it was time for me to leave, she told me to return sooner than
later and gave me a hug. I went to her home again for her sixty-
seventh birthday party. She and I danced together, her arms reaching
high to grasp my tall shoulders. She was so incredibly happy. Her
contagious smile was framed by her gray-and-white, straight long
hair. It lit up the room, which was filled more with human beings than
with decorations.

I wrote María the following letter not long after first embracing
her. I'm not sure why I wrote it, and why I never gave it to her. Maybe
it was because I wanted to understand the tension she was living in,
maybe because I wondered what I would do if my son decided not to
live a religious life, maybe because her son made such an impact on
me. And I knew a huge part of that impact was a direct reflection of
her influence.

Dear María,

I admire my own mother for many things, mostly for her belief
in her children. Very often we do not agree on the decisions I
make for my life. But the bond between a mother and her child
is strong—something I have yet to fully understand from the
other side.

I know you know that your son loves you, but maybe you will
never know exactly how much he admires you. You are often on
his lips, and your consistency in your beliefs paralleled with
your hard work shows him something he cannot quite grasp—
not yet. You have created a beautiful man who seeks to do the

right thing. He believes God exists because of you, and I hope one day you will see just how influential your faith has been on his life. I think one of the most amazing qualities about God is that we can find him wherever we are. Just as you find him in the eyes of a stranger, in the walls of your church, and in the words of the priest's mouth; your son finds him in the daily work of your hands, in the walls of your house, and in the words of your mouth.

The beauty of Christ is how he transcends everything our human hands try to place him in. He is more powerful, more majestic, more mysterious, more loving. He is capable of forgiving so many things, and he is capable of using us in so many ways.

Don't stop praying for Elí. Don't stop doing what he says you do best: seeing God in everyone. You are more of an inspiration than you know. May you see the face of God, may you feel his touch, may you sense his presence in the everyday normalcies of life.

María was Catholic. But she wasn't the kind of Catholic I'd heard about during my evangelical upbringing. She was deeply in love with Christ, attended church regularly, visited the sick and the incarcerated. María was the type of Catholic I saw in two of my favorite Italian relatives; they loved Christ profoundly and fought their whole lives for the rights of the marginalized. María paved a way for me to see that Zizi Grace and Uncle Bear weren't anomalies in the Catholic faith. It was then I started rejecting the evangelical suggestions that Catholics are somehow inferior Christians.

BEING A SINGLE AMERICAN WOMAN

"Getting married here is not like you think. It's not the same as getting married in the States," Adriana told me as we were running an errand together to get my apartment situated. "We expect our husbands to cheat on us." I could hardly believe that was her reality. She was married. She had three young children.

I often came to family dinners and hung out with her extended family, including brothers and cousins—some married, some not. They all felt like family to me. I was comfortable around all of them. "Be careful," she said to me, and I started adjusting my comfort level around men.

A few weeks later, her married cousin was driving me on another errand, as he often helped us American teachers. He had picked me up from the airport a few times, and we ran errands for the school together. When he dropped me off at my apartment, he moved closer in the seat of the truck, leaned in, and tried to kiss me. I pushed him away, got out of the truck, and went into my apartment.

I don't remember if I said anything. I don't remember details. I remember only feelings: betrayal, frustration, confusion, anger at him, at the culture, at the knowledge that this was normal, at myself for any signals I'd sent that would invite that.

I taught his daughter. I was friends with his wife, and I didn't know what to tell her. I didn't know how to tell anyone. So I didn't say a word. Instead I did everything I could to protect myself from being with him at all—and especially alone.

Fast-forward several months. I had been enjoying hanging out with the *mara*. We would go to bars and talk into the early morning. Beer was not appealing to me, so I would enjoy conversation with a Coke or a water. Every once in a while, I'd drink a rum and Coke. We cooked meals at each other's houses, listened to bachata music, and planned camping adventures. Some of the guys had girlfriends; some didn't. Some of the Americans and the Hondurans began dating each other. Elí Romero had a girlfriend who never came around to these events, but I had met her in other settings. Nacho had a girlfriend, but she never came around, so I never met her.

One night, Nacho walked me home. Then he kissed me, and I kissed back.

Even if he had been drinking, I hadn't. So why did I do it? Was it because I was feeling lonely? Was it because I wanted to fit in with the rest of the *mara*?

He wanted to come into my apartment. I said no, and thankfully he listened.

I was so mad at myself. Adriana's words had hit again: this time like a corrective slap to the face. This wasn't a Honduran problem; it was a universal problem that I had just contributed to.

My journal was full of confusion. Full of prayers. Full of searching.

Lord, this is not the person I want to be. I don't want to tell anyone, because I am so scared of what other people think of me. I know to a certain degree that this is part of human nature, and therefore natural—but that justification only makes it worse, because sin then becomes a normality. But this really hurts the heart of Christ. In the moment, the power of the cross was not as powerful as the desire. I don't want to be this person. I don't like who I am. Please, Lord, let your blood wash over me.

I was baptized in elementary school. I was a good kid, rarely in trouble, always following the rules. So when the pastor dunked me under and said I would arise to a new life in Christ, I didn't actually understand. My life had always been with Christ. I never knew a day without him. I didn't have a lot of visual sins in my past to look back on.

Baptism pushes you deep into the waters. In Honduras, I understood those deep waters. I was deep in the waters of losing myself, questioning my identity, questioning my community. I swam in those deep waters longer than I want to admit. I was lonely and afraid. I felt like my spiritual life was drowning. But some of us have to lose our bearings, our identity, our comfort, before we realize we don't want to gain the whole world.

And in the moment of letting the world go, we are lifted out of the deep waters as a new creation—with a former self that we may not be proud of but that we are no longer afraid of. True salvation, true wholeness, comes first by realizing our true humanity—not only what we have done but what we are capable of doing. We won't look for a doctor if we are blind to our sicknesses. We don't need a savior if we own the rescue boat.

The process of losing myself and questioning my identity brought me to a profound understanding of God's grace that I hadn't grasped as a former goody two-shoes. And the Lord gave me an amazing sister, Monique, to walk through it with me. She worked at the bilingual Christian school not far from the school I worked at. We had deep conversations about God, the struggle to indulge in our desires, the hope we had for our future. We talked about men, about family, about living as American women in Honduras. We hung out with other expats and with Hondurans. We went dancing together, did Bible study together, and camped together. She had her own struggles with life in Honduras and confided in me. I never felt judged by her, though she constantly challenged me to be more like Christ. I thank God when I remember her. She showed me a Christianity that offers space for my humanity.

This internal experience in Honduras prepared me for Julia's presence in our home more than living in Honduras ever could. Fostering can easily be done from a mindset of charity: "I have something you need, and I'll sacrifice to give it to you because I'm a good person." My experience ripped that option from me. Now I know that any call I think I have must be balanced with the tension of my identity as both the worst sinner and the daughter of the King. I can't do what I'm called to do because I'm better than, or because I have more than, or because I can be a good example to "those" people.

Biblical justice doesn't let me get away with motivations that set me on a pedestal. It shows me my sin—and all the sin I'm capable of committing. Actually having actions to regret in life ironically gave me the experience I needed to see that foster care isn't what I do to sacrificially give of my good self; rather, it's a system I get involved in with all my humanity in tow, learning to sacrifice the angel I imagine myself to be.

Any calling we follow in attempts to rid the world of injustice is not a call for us to be saviors of the world or saviors of our neighbors or even saviors of ourselves. I arrived in Honduras with a false identity: my goodness is pedestal-worthy. I left knowing better.

PART 2

MEXICO

UNITED STATES

McAllen, Texas

Mexico City

MEXICO

BELIZE

Tela

HONDURAS

GUATEMALA

EL SALVADOR

NICARAGUA

COSTA RICA

Chapter Three

RÍO BRAVO

LUPE AND JULIA: 2017

Warning: parts of this chapter are inescapably violent and disturbing.

INTO MEXICO

In AD 427, Mayan leader Yax K'uk' Mo migrated from the Guatemalan highlands into the Copan valley of Honduras. There his dynasty of sixteen rulers transformed Copan, creating one of the greatest Mayan cities.[1] More than 1,500 years later, Lupe, Julia, and Carlos traveled northwest to Copan in October 2017, reversing the path Yax K'uk' Mo had taken. Feeling vulnerable yet hopeful, they met their ruthless leader, Luciana, a *coyota* (female smuggler) who had been creating her own type of dynasty.

Lupe thought, *I'm only here because I'm desperate. I need to save my grandfather's life and give my children a better future.*

But her cousin's friends, who had recommended Luciana, hadn't told Lupe what type of person Luciana was. She thought she could trust their judgment. She thought that she, Carlos, and Julia would be in good hands. Of course, she knew the risk of what often happens to women: they are held for ransom, forced to be drug mules, raped, or killed. But Carlos was with them, and the *coyota* had been recommended by a friend who'd had no major trouble arriving in the United States.

Lupe's nerves accompanied her on her ride to Copan. *Even if I am kidnapped or sold, because of Carlos's stepdad status, he will take care of Julia,* she thought, trying to calm her fears.

"The American dream is very difficult," Luciana told them. "Whether you cross the border or you return to your hometown, you still owe me the money." Lupe and Carlos had already given her the first installment of two thousand dollars. By the end, they would pay a total of seventy-five hundred to Luciana.

"God protect me and my daughter," Lupe prayed after Luciana's fear-inducing talk to the crowd of migrants.

Luciana was already choosing who she would get to run her errands. Lupe was one of the chosen. Before Luciana left the crowd in her own car, she spoke to Marcos, her right-hand man, who was called El Guía, The Guide. As she spoke, she looked at the group and said, "You know what to do if certain migrants don't behave."

That night, the group, which consisted of forty adults and thirty-five children, crossed the Honduran border into Guatemala. Two days later, Luciana returned to the group and separated Lupe from Julia— who was five years old at the time—and said she had a job for Lupe to do. "You aren't allowed to ask any questions," Luciana said, handing Lupe a backpack. "Get on the bus that will be stationed at Rampa 4."

But that day, no bus arrived. The group continued to move on, and although Lupe didn't have to run Luciana's errand, she had been targeted and kept separate from Julia. Other mothers in the group were taking care of Julia. The next day, the group arrived in Mexico City.

"Can I see my daughter?" Lupe desperately asked again and again. Annoyed, Luciana responded, "Now you will enter your Calvary." During the day, Lupe was with Julia, but at night, she worked for Luciana at her night club. She didn't sleep for four days. She was forced to put on a lot of makeup. She was forced to prostitute herself.

Lupe said she suffered a lot during that time, and she refrained from giving details. She said she wished she could forget the horror she lived through.

THE HORRORS OF MIGRANT ABUSE

In an attempt to better understand what Lupe went through, below is a paragraph from Shanthi Sekaran's fictional piece *Lucky Boy*, in which one of the main characters, Soli, is raped at gunpoint by three men smuggling her across the border. If you have been a victim of sexual harassment or assault, skip over this section. My desire here is to give depth to words and situations that can be glazed over because sitting in another's pain is too costly or foreign to us.

Soli had told no one about those men, and would have wiped her memory clean if she could. But she couldn't. Three men. Three cowboy hats, all white, like they'd bought them together. They'd used her like a latrine, taking turns, each moving methodically like a dog f—ing a dog. By the time the third had jammed himself inside her, she could stare into the sun's glare and think of herself as a dog, and them as dogs, and nothing more. When all of them were animals, the spikes of pain deadened and she felt nothing. She'd felt nothing when they ground her shoulders into the dirt. She'd felt nothing when the third man held a knife to her throat, smiled, and pulled the blade away.[2]

Lupe's story is different from Soli's, but both were treated inhumanely and stripped of their dignity. Tragically, many migrant women share similar stories. In Mexico, an estimated 341,000 people live in modern-day slavery.[3] According the Migration Policy Institute,

Women face extreme hardship on the journey northward, as they experience disproportionately high rates of sexual violence, and can be victimized by actors such as smugglers (coyotes), gangs, cartels, and police. Despite these dangers, growing numbers of Central American women have set off through Mexico in recent years.[4]

And the sexual abuse doesn't stop at the US border. Many immigrant women suffer sexual abuse and labor exploitation after entering the United States, where the threat of deportation is used by partners, employers, and traffickers.

One night, Lupe overhead Luciana and Marcos talking at the nightclub. "Lupe is making me a lot of money," Luciana told him. "Maybe I'll keep her here."

"But Lupe still owes you more money for the trip," Marcos said. "If you leave her here, you won't get the other installments of her money."

"In Reynosa, I will make more money with Lupe. I'll make her do everything I want her to do."

The next day, Lupe was taken back to the group. They all got on a bus and were driven to a new location. They got off the bus and were split up into several sedans. Lupe was separated again from Julia.

Lupe was told to get in one of the cars with a man she recognized from the nightclub. "You are going to do whatever he tells you," Luciana told Lupe, and she did.

Every time Lupe was moved from one place to another, it was new territory for her. She was told no details, only given orders.

"Your desert begins now," Luciana told her when she arrived at two semi-trailer trucks, where her group had joined with other groups. As bleak as the future looked, Lupe was grateful to be reunited with Julia.

INTO THE EIGHTEEN-WHEELER

More than two hundred people were in each trailer, the majority of them women and children. The women sat on the edge of the trailer, all squeezed together. The men sat in a single-file line in the middle.

"You each get three apples and one liter of water," said a male smuggler in charge as he passed out the rations. "Children get two bottles of Pedialyte."

The group was soon to be on the move toward Reynosa in a sweaty, dark, fifty-by-eight-foot metal box.

As the journey began, so did the hostility. "I need water!" a migrant called out in the darkness.

"Shut up, or we'll kill you!" the smugglers snapped back.

The female migrants feared sexual abuse by the smugglers, and the male migrants feared physical abuse. Threats were made if silence was not kept. Sunlight was absent. Two buckets on opposite sides of the trailer served as latrines—one for males, the other for females. The darkness was cut open only when the smugglers turned on their cell phones or flashlights.

The smugglers used drugs in the trailer. Women were raped. Each time they came for Lupe to rape her, she left Julia with Miriam, a young woman who had showed Julia affection.

I must accept everything that happens to me here, Lupe thought. *There is no other option. Men are miserable creatures.*

The high desert of Mexico is hot during the day and cold at night during the fall months, so the temperature inside the trailer was very hot during the day and very cold at night. Any time the truck driver turned off the engine, the air stopped circulating in the trailer, causing it to swell with heat. When the driver cranked the truck, the ventilation system sucked the air out of the trailer.

As the air was sucked out of the trailer, children and pregnant women whimpered and fainted while many of the men kicked and pounded the walls. The smugglers took out their weapons to gain control.

At one point, Julia began crying at the sound of the guns. "Hush!" said one of the guards as he covered her mouth, preventing her from breathing. She fainted into Lupe's arms.

On the front end of the trailer was a father and mother with a nine-month-old baby. The baby cried and cried, causing the smugglers' anger and frustration to escalate. The mother was worried the baby was dying.

A very drugged smuggler said, "Let's shoot the baby." Lupe spoke up, saying, "Bring the baby to me. I'll feed it." Then she immediately

LIFE AND DEATH IN THE TRAILERS

In 2003, eighteen migrants, including an infant, suffocated to death in the back of a semi-trailer.[5]

In 2017, ten men had died when authorities discovered thirty-nine people in a semi in San Antonio.[6]

In 2017, Univision collected more than 150 stories from Latinos who migrated to the United States in tractor-trailers. One of those stories is from Jose Ernesto Peña, who said,

> I traveled the whole way through Mexico in a truck, in four different trucks. In the one from Puebla to Zacatecas we were 243 people. It was a 52-foot tractor-trailer, one of the longest ones, that usually carries meats, fruits. It's supposed to be cool inside but the air-conditioning had broken and we almost died from lack of oxygen. It reminded me of a movie, *The Death Truck* (*El Camión de la Muerte*), where immigrants die. That's how it is. You see death close. The smell is horrible: people haven't bathed, rotten feet, armpits, bad breath, people going to the bathroom. The oxygen is bad. You're not even breathing oxygen—it's something else. The body wants to pass out. When we arrived at the ranch and they opened the door so we could get out, the way people left . . . it's not like when people leave the stadium. It was an avalanche of people.[7]

said a prayer, "God, fill up my breasts so I can feed this baby and my daughter."

The smuggler brought Lupe the baby. She held Julia in one arm and the baby boy in the other. Miraculously, her breasts began to fill. As each breast was suckled by children who desperately needed the nutrients, Lupe knew God had heard her prayer. She felt strong for the first time on the journey.

But Julia continued to suffer. About an hour before arriving in Reynosa, she had lost a lot of strength, so Lupe returned the baby to his mother, saying, "I just can't take care of them both." The baby began crying again, and Julia fainted again.

Not long before the trip ended, the trailer suddenly turned off because the driver had seen airplanes overhead. Once again, the lack of air circulation gave way to chaos. Men and women hit themselves and the trailer walls. The smuggler in charge got angry, saying things like, "If you keep doing this, I will assassinate some of you! I don't care where you are from!"

Lupe and Miriam prayed and prayed that no one would die.

After arriving in Reynosa and exiting the trailer, one of the smugglers received a call from Luciana. He then walked up to Lupe. "Luciana wants to see you."

She left her suitcase and Julia with Miriam and made her way to where Luciana was. *I'm going to lose Julia*, she thought as she approached the woman who would decide her fate.

Luciana told her the plan. "Your daughter will go in the truck, and you will stay here."

So Lupe told Miriam to take care of Julia for her. "I know I'm never going to see her again. Take care of her as you go through Customs and Immigration."

Carlos overheard Lupe talking, and he asked one of the smugglers, "Why does Lupe have to stay here if the three of us came together?" The smuggler ignored his question just as the other smugglers had ignored his myriad of other questions on the trip north.

As Miriam got off the trailer with Julia, Lupe tried reaching out for Julia. Miriam stopped her, saying, "Don't do it. They will kill you."

"I don't care if they do. Stay with my daughter."

"I will take care of her. Don't worry."

When one of the smugglers saw Lupe reaching out, he said, "If you try to leave or scream, I will shoot you."

The strength Lupe had felt when her breasts filled with milk was fully stripped from her now. She knew they would try to squeeze more money out of her. She knew she was walking away from motherhood and into prostitution and drug smuggling. She knew that Luciana had her right where she wanted her.

Luciana walked up to Lupe and said, "Your drama ends here." Julia sobbed with shaking shoulders and dangling arms as Miriam carried her away from her mother. Lupe kept her eyes on Julia as long as she could. She saw one of the smugglers kindly give her a piece of pizza and a cup of orange juice.

Lupe had little hope she'd see Julia again.

MIGRANTS AS COMMODITIES

Increasing smuggling fees is a common tactic. Francisco Cantú reported in his book, *The Line Becomes a River*,

> As border crossings became more difficult, traffickers increased their smuggling fees. In turn, as smuggling became more profitable, it was increasingly consolidated under the regional operations of the drug cartels. Every surge in border enforcement has brought a corresponding increase to the yield potential of each perspective migrant. For smuggling gangs, holding clients for ransom is a simple way of maximizing profit. Matthew Allen, the senior agent in charge of the US Immigration and Customs Enforcement office in Phoenix, put it succinctly: ". . . The alien becomes a commodity. . . . One way you raise the value of that commodity is by threatening [and] terrorizing someone."[8]

LA BODEGA (THE WAREHOUSE)

One of the smugglers whipped out a fabric bag, put it over Lupe's face, and drove her to a bodega, a warehouse-like building. On the way there, another gave her food. "Eat, and eat a lot," he said. "You will be working hard, moving drugs from one side of the border to the other."

But Lupe wasn't hungry. "Tell me what you did with my daughter? Is she okay, or are you going to sell her to a cartel?" She threw herself onto him, pleading, "Kill me, *maldito* (damned one)."

"You will suffer, bitch," he said before he hit her.

Lupe saw that she was there with five other women being held hostage. Just as in the trailer, she stayed awake at night out of fear.

The next day, she was introduced to a man from Guatemala who told her, "Luciana wants to see you."

"I don't care. I need to know where my daughter is."

"I know your heart is broken, and I'm really sorry if your family doesn't help you. They will kill your daughter or fill her with drugs. But listen, Lupe, be strong. You are still alive."

In a sedan, he drove Lupe to the place where Julia was. All the children were sitting with their mothers on the bank of the river. Lupe was able to see that Julia was okay and that she was with Carlos.

Miriam approached Lupe and said, "We're going to cross the river, and I believe you are going to come too, Lupe."

The Guatemalan driver then took Lupe to see Luciana. "Thank you," Lupe said to Luciana. "I will thank you the rest of my life."

"But you aren't going in the same boat your daughter is going in," Luciana replied.

As the rest of the group got into the boat, it was clear she was not going anywhere. "What about me?" Lupe asked.

"You will stay here."

"Kill me then. I don't want to be alive any longer."

Luciana punched Lupe's face several times, and Lupe felt the warmth of blood as her hand instinctively nursed her wounds. Then she said, "Who are you hitting? I don't feel anything."

"You're an animal. One of these days, I'll do something to you that you'll remember your whole life."

"Everything that has happened to me I will never forget if I live to remember."

Lupe was taken back to the bodega, and one of Luciana's workers tied her hands behind her back. She then suffered similar wounds to her face at the hands of her captors. With a puffy face and a purple body, Lupe lay on the cold cement floor. There she slept for the first time in several nights.

The next morning two men threw a bucket of cold water on her.

"God, why have you forgotten me?" she said aloud.

"We are your god now," one of the men said.

Any time the captors came toward her, Lupe knew she was about to get a beating. "What do you want from me?" she'd ask. Instead of answering her, the men hit her. Then they took photos of her—specifically photos of the wounds they'd inflicted. Lupe would never know why they took the pictures or to whom they were being sent.

Sometimes they would rape her. Sometimes she would be sent away to get raped, further lining Luciana's pockets.

For six days in the bodega, Lupe received no food. Marcos, the main guide, arrived on a Friday and said, "You'll be leaving here soon. And when I return, I'll bring you good news."

"The only good news you can bring me is to tell me right now where my daughter is."

"She's alive, Lupe. She's with the gringos in the United States," Marcos said.

"I don't believe you," Lupe replied, thinking they had sold Julia. "I want proof of life."

Marcos showed Lupe a video of Julia and Carlos crossing the river while a Border Patrol officer walked up to them along with the others who were in their crowd and took them into custody.

"When Luciana shows up, Lupe, you need to stay calm, because she's particularly furious with you because Border Patrol is going to keep the girl, even though they deported Carlos the day after he arrived. Stay calm, Lupe, because they can kill you."

"Thank you for telling me," Lupe replied.

Several days later, for the first time Lupe's hands were untied, and she was taken to a bar. She was given back her telephone momentarily and allowed to talk to Marta, Carlos's sister, who was in North Carolina. "Marta, they are holding me hostage here," Lupe said. "They want more money."

"Everything is going to be fine. Julia is here with me," Marta replied. "You'll be able to escape."

Luciana came in and hung up the phone, cutting short their conversation, and then backhanded Lupe across the face. "Today is the day your daughter will die," Luciana said, but Lupe knew that would be difficult even for Luciana. Perceiving that, Luciana tried a different tactic. "I will go to Honduras and get your sons." That scared Lupe because she knew it was possible.

Luciana began looking through Lupe's telephone. Lupe had sent a message to her aunt Raquel, telling her there was about 830 US dollars in her bank account and that only Raquel had the ability to take it out of the account.

Luciana saw the message, and Lupe was taken back to the bodega. As she was unable to sleep that night, Lupe's head swirled with questions: *Will Raquel hand over the money to Luciana? Will Luciana threaten Julia again? Will she find out where my boys are living?*

The next day, Luciana had news for Lupe. "Look, bitch. They are depositing the twenty thousand lempiras from your bank account into mine. Your sweat, my luck. How many years did you work for that sum of money? In one day, it's all mine."

"It doesn't matter to me," Lupe said. "Take it."

"Tomorrow I'm going to get Border Patrol to deport Julia," Luciana said. "You will never have anything ever again. And tonight I'm going to sell you off to the most revolting man in the world."

At two in the morning, Luciana's latter promise came through.

"God please give me strength," Lupe prayed as she was given over to a large, smiling man.

The man grabbed her hand and said, "This is your day."

"Do as you wish," she said.

The man bruised and beat and raped Lupe. Hours later, Luciana came and had her men sew up one of Lupe's wounds—five stitches in her side and no anesthesia. The scar would never let her forget.

She was taken back to the bodega. The stench of the Most Revolting Man stayed on her.

Weeks passed. She would be beaten, raped, beaten, and raped again. The wound on her side didn't heal. She and the other women were told to strip naked in front of the male captors.

Lupe began planning her escape, but the bodega was full of traps. The men who worked there were free to rape Lupe whenever they wanted.

One of the guards, Victor, didn't have feet and had only one functioning hand. In his good hand, he always held a pistol. When he was on guard, he was accompanied by another guard, who was constantly shooting up. One day, Lupe asked Victor, "Don't you have a family or daughters?"

"Yes, that's why I work here, so I can give them food to eat."

"That's awful. Let me go. What do you want from me?" she said. "They're going to kill me. Do you want them to kill me?"

"I want to help you, but you have to wait until the other guard leaves," Victor replied.

When the drug addict left, Victor called for Lupe and then said, "If you give me a piece of your body, I will help you escape."

"But I'm wounded," Lupe responded, looking down at her shirt, where the pus was being absorbed.

"It doesn't matter. Do you want to make the deal or not?"

Considering her depleting strength and wondering if she'd have any other options for escape, Lupe made the deal with Victor. That same night, he helped her escape. Dehydrated, bruised, and wounded, Lupe began a staggering walk in her shorts and T-shirt in forty-five-degree Fahrenheit weather and continued walking into the morning.

A taxi came by. "Do you want a ride?"

"Please take me anywhere but here," she told him.

"If you have money, I can take you."

"Look at me. I'm wounded. Please help me! I'm afraid. I'm not from here."

"Wow, you are very beat up and wounded!" he said. "I'll help you."

Lupe knew she'd never forget that moment. She didn't realize until it had happened that she had nearly lost hope that anyone would ever help her again.

"Can you take me to Migración?" she asked.

He took Lupe to an area where she could easily reach Mexican migration officials. As she walked toward the migration office, an elderly woman, Minerva, stopped and gave Lupe a hug. "I'm so sorry there are so many delinquents here in my country," she said. "I will help you." Minerva repeated herself, shouting this time. "I will help you!"

Lupe was concerned that the Reynosa townspeople would think she was a *coyota*. But they didn't. There were good people in Reynosa, people who hugged her, gave her bus money, and asked her what had happened.

Minerva took Lupe to her house. On the way there, she called her family to tell them about Lupe. When they arrived at Minerva's house, there were towels stacked out, welcoming Lupe to bathe. Minerva gathered some plant leaves and began making tea for Lupe while she cleaned up.

Minerva saw that one of Lupe's wounds was infected and gaping open. She gathered gauze and bandages and did what she could to cover it. It hurt, but the comfort of Minerva's home gave Lupe a peace that covered the physical pain she felt.

That peace began to slip away when Lupe called her family back in Honduras. Reality hit extra hard when she called her aunt, who reminded her she had given all her money to Luciana.

"Lupe! Your grandfather is sick. Agonizingly sick. He won't make it much longer," Raquel added.

Lupe's heart sank. She remembered Luciana's words—This is your Calvary—and thought, *My Calvary isn't over yet.*

She hung up the phone. She thought about how Julia needed her, but Julia was in the United States with Marta. And she had no money to get there and no papers to present. She thought about how her grandfather, who she'd cared for her whole life, needed her. If she went to a Mexican Migración office, they would send her back to Honduras.

"Minerva, please take me to Migración," she said. Minerva quickly obliged.

When they arrived at the office prior to entering, Lupe called Raquel one more time. Raquel said, "He's dying."

Lupe's world seemed to be spinning. The whole trip had been to get enough money to buy his medicine so he would be able to live. Her daughter had been separated from her. Her body and spirit were broken, her bank account robbed. And now her grandfather was on his deathbed.

Lupe hugged Minerva goodbye and thanked her for her kindness. "I don't know how I can ever repay you," she said.

"My daughter, you don't have to."

Lupe entered Migración, where they began the process for her deportation back to Honduras. They admitted her to their health clinic and gave her much-needed medicine.

"We have some news," a Migración official told her a week later while her paperwork was still being processed. "Brace yourself."

Lupe knew what was coming.

"Your grandfather is dead."

ARRIVING HOME

Not long after El Día de San Valentín (Valentine's Day), Lupe stepped off the bus that had taken her from Reynosa, Mexico, to San Pedro

Sula, Honduras. She then got on another local bus. The last hours of her journey would take her home to her little town and her rented house, which used to have seven family members under one roof. Now it would be five. The guilt of that sat heavy with her.

Upon arrival, all three boys ran up to Lupe and hugged her and began crying. "Abuelo is dead," they each told her. Immediately she felt guilty that she hadn't been there to comfort them when he passed. Her grandmother, rather than embracing her, was frozen stiff, sitting on the worn-out maroon armchair in the living room. Silent. She stayed that way for hours.

The next day, Raquel arrived. "This is all your fault," she said. "My father is dead because you left!" But Lupe knew that it was Raquel's own neglect of her father's needs that was to blame. She also knew then and there that she would never be able to talk about what had happened to her in Mexico.

Her neighbors piled on the same guilt. "Your grandfather is dead because you left."

She felt guilty for Julia's absence, and she had no idea if reunification was possible.

She felt guilty for her grandfather's death.

She felt guilty for not being there for her boys.

She felt guilty for not being there for her grandmother.

She felt guilty for everything that had happened to her in Mexico.

She felt guilty for the failure of her body, the depression of her spirit—guilty that she had been raped so many times because of a poor choice she made.

Guilt seemed to be her only companion. So she started drinking. She drank and drank to drown out the nightmares of life.

Abel, an old friend, came to see her a few weeks after she had returned home. "You have to stop drinking," he told her.

"I have suffered so much," she responded, but she gave no details of her suffering. Abel thought she was talking simply about her grandfather's death and her separation from Julia.

"If you don't stop drinking, you will die, and no one will take care of the children who are here with you."

She knew it was true. She sobered up, got her old job at the tortilla factory back, and worked two shifts a day. She started attending church and found minute comforts in the regular routines of life.

A little more than three weeks after she arrived, she video-chatted with a white American family in North Carolina. Julia had just moved in with them.

Chapter Four

RIO GRANDE

GENA AND FAMILY: 2009–2013

BIASES BETWEEN MEXICO AND CENTRAL AMERICA

Not long after I moved home from Honduras, I reconnected with Andrew. He and I had played soccer at Central Cabarrus High School in North Carolina. Grown-up Andrew was mysterious to me. He was living in a tent deep in the mountains, working at a sawmill. His burly beard, long brown hair, and sense of adventure swept me away. Flannels were an essential part of his wardrobe and gave him the quintessential mountain-man look.

Andrew's love for nature was refreshing. When we went hiking, he told me the types of trees we were passing. He introduced me to rock climbing, a sport I'd never intended to experience. Atop a three-pitch route, I was unable to hold in my fearful sobs. When my tears and consequential anger didn't push him away, I had a feeling we would be teammates for life.

At twenty-three, and after my experiences in Honduras, I wasn't interested in dating for fun, and I was up front with Andrew about that. He felt the same way, and within four months, we were engaged. About a year after getting engaged, we nervously said our vows to each other in front of about twenty of our family members.

We decided that by the time we were celebrating our one-year anniversary, we'd be actively seeking jobs overseas if no opportunity had already come up. The thought of being in the Peace Corps tugged on us both. But a month after we married, missionaries I had lived with in Nicaragua for a few months during college moved to Mexico and emailed me, saying, "We're looking for English teachers for the middle school that's starting in August. Pray about it."

Don't need to, I thought. *Not happening.*

I had lived in Nicaragua, traveled through every country in Central America, and been back to "Nica" several times since. I had also lived fifteen months in Honduras. I had never once been to Mexico. In college, my Spanish minor had me on track to take a course on Mexico, but when I decided to take a semester off and live in Nicaragua, the course on Spain was the only one available to me before graduating. I felt relieved, and I loved learning about Spain. Mexico was the bad guy in my head, and I'm not sure I knew why.

In light of immigration, I'd like to discuss this negative bias regarding Mexico that seeped into my subconscious. My perception of this is based solely on my experiences and my research. It isn't everyone's perspective, and it certainly isn't the whole truth.

In her book *Tell Me How It Ends*, Valeria Luiselli, a Mexican author living in the United States, pointed to this bias several times. She worked as an interpreter in the New York immigration court, where she performed intake interviews with unaccompanied minors.

Question seven on the questionnaire was "Did anything happen on your trip to the United States that scared you or hurt you?" The children seldom gave details of their experiences along the journey through Mexico upon a first screening, and it wasn't necessarily useful to push them for more information. What happens to them between their home countries and their arrival in the United States couldn't always help their defense before an immigration judge, so the question didn't make up a substantial part of the interview. But, as a Mexican, this is the question I feel most ashamed of, because what happens to children during their journey through Mexico is always worse than what happens anywhere else.

The numbers tell horror stories.

Rapes. Eighty percent of the women and girls who cross Mexico to get to the US border are raped on the way.[1] It is so common that most of them take contraceptive precautions as they begin the journey north.

Abductions. In 2011, the National Human Rights Commission in Mexico published a special report on immigrant abductions and kidnappings, revealing that the number of abduction victims between April and September 2010—a period of just six months—was 11,333.

Deaths and disappearances. Though it's impossible to establish an actual number, some sources estimate that, since 2006, about 120,000 migrants have disappeared in their transit through Mexico.

Beyond the terrifying but abstract statistics, many horror stories have recently tattooed themselves on the collective social conscience of Mexico.[2]

Luiselli outlines the first intake interview she gave to a sixteen-year-old boy, Manu, from Honduras.

Why did you come to the United States?

He says nothing and looks at me, shrugs a little. I reassure him:

I'm not policewoman, I'm no official anyone. I'm not even a lawyer. I'm also not a gringa, you know? In fact, I can't help you at all. But I can't hurt you, either.

So why are *you* here then?

I'm just here to translate for you.

And what are you?

What do you mean?

I mean: where are you from?

I'm a *chilanga*.

Well, I'm a *catracho*, so we're enemies.

He's right: I'm from Mexico City and he's from Honduras, and in many ways, that makes us hostile neighbors.[3]

A 2012 CNN article reported the closing of a Catholic-run immigrant house near Mexico City after violence broke out in the town.

Immigrant rights advocates described it as a significant setback, warning that long-simmering xenophobia toward Central American immigrants in the area had reached a boiling point.

"They face racial discrimination and social exclusion," Mexico City's Human Rights Commission said in a statement.

"Mexico is repeating the immigration policy of the United States. If we don't look at ourselves critically, we could fall into the same trap," said Raul Vera Lopez, a Catholic bishop in the northern city of Saltillo, according to Mexico's state-run Notimex news agency.[4]

Not all Mexicans are xenophobic toward Central Americans, just as not all American Christians are xenophobic toward immigrants. Las Patronas, a formal humanitarian group, started when a group of women from La Patrona, in the state of Veracruz, Mexico, threw bottled water and food to migrants aboard the infamous train(s)[5] nicknamed La Bestia (The Beast) that many migrants ride up through Mexico to get to the United States.[6] In fact, in the state of Veracruz, "The towns of Encinar, Fortín de las Fores, Cuichapa, and Presidio are particularly known for their kindness" among migrants.[7] There are many Catholic leaders, such as Father Lopez in the above CNN story, Father Alejandro Solalinde, Bishop Hipolito Reyes Larios, Father Salamon Lemus Lemus, and many townspeople and volunteers who counterculturally fight for the dignity of migrants. Bishop Larios said, "One of the acts of mercy is to give shelter to a migrant."[8]

Mexico was not a land I ever imagined I'd live in, let alone become a mother in. When the opportunity to move to Mexico came up, I had to face my own bias. Would the hierarchy I had created in my head that said Mexico was bad (the oppressor) and Central America was good (the oppressed) stop me, a white American oppressor (arguably at the top of the hierarchy of oppressors) from following the God who calls down all hierarchies?

The older I get, the more I see God doing just that—calling down hierarchies. There is no label that God considers more worthy than another. But we assume this all the time: The Protestant is better than the Catholic. The boy is better than the girl. The missionary is better than the person in the pew.

God reluctantly gave the Israelites a king after trying to convince them they didn't need such a hierarchy. Undeniably hierarchies give us a false sense of control. But the gospel wipes out hierarchies as *all* have fallen short. All are in need of a Savior. All must recognize the sin they are capable of, even if they have the purest-looking public life.

I'm not going to say that as soon as Andrew and I felt God calling us to Mexico, I laid down my bias. I did not. I deeply struggled to live in Mexico during our first year there. It was probably the worst year of my adult life for many reasons. But struggle often produces a special kind of fruit, and I'm still reaping a harvest from my personal issues and idols that surfaced that first year.

At month seven of our marriage, in August 2009, Andrew and I hitched his six-by-twelve-foot landscape trailer to his 1997 Isuzu Rodeo and drove thirty-five hours to El Carmen, Nuevo Laredo, Mexico. When we got to the border in Laredo, Texas, we were stopped briefly by Mexican border agents.

"*Pasaportes,*" an agent said, holding out his hand to receive our privileged papers. "Where are you going?" he asked, looking at us, then peering into our backseat, and then scanning our trailer.

"El Carmen," Andrew responded.

"What are you going to do?"

"We'll be teaching English."

The agent told us to get out of the Rodeo and asked us to pull the tarp off what was stored in the trailer. Then he and his colleague had us take off one box at a time so they could look through all of our cargo. An hour later, we were on our way to our new home.

Our three-day journey that August was the beginning of a whole new phase and a whole new perspective. We had no idea how familiar we would become with Laredo, Texas, and the border-crossing process there. Over the years, we learned to dress nicely on our trips into the United States so US Customs and Border Protection Officers (CBPOs) wouldn't think we were hippies smuggling marijuana. We learned to take off our sunglasses and hats, roll down our backseat windows, and not be alarmed by the drug dogs and the long-poled mirrors used to look at the wheel wells of our car.

Though we always had a lot of errands to run in Laredo, we knew to budget extra time in case CBPOs stopped us. We also learned that some of our Mexican friends had Border Crossing Cards that allowed them to travel only twenty-five miles north of the border. So they couldn't pass legally at the checkpoint north of town. But Andrew and I easily moved through with our American passports.

On one of our trips, I leaned my forehead against the passenger window, looking at the brown Rio Grande as we neared Laredo and wondered about how some of our Mexican friends would cross the river to get to where we were going in our air-conditioned car. Scenes from the 2007 National Geographic documentary *Wetback: The Undocumented Documentary* crossed my mind. *Mojado*[9] is a word that I, as a white American, would never say out loud, but it's one I heard a lot when neighbors told me third-person accounts of successful and failed attempts to be immigrants in the land that defined so much of my own identity, the land I had just left easily and could easily return to at any time.

Concern about what my Honduran friends would think when they found out about my move increased to angst. But long into my life three hours south of Laredo, I became aware of a strong biblical truth buried in a somewhat depressing book of the Old Testament. One of the richest men who ever lived said, "The race is not to the swift, nor the battle to the strong, nor bread to the wise, nor riches to the intelligent, nor favor to those with knowledge, but time and chance happen to them all" (Ecclesiastes 9:11 ESV). Bias or no bias, life in Mexico is similar to life in Honduras and life in the United States; no matter where they are, human beings seek out better circumstances for themselves and for their families. In each land are oppressors and oppressed, oppressors who were oppressed themselves, and many who vacillate between the two. In each land are people who disregard the humanity of others. In each land are pockets of people living counterculturally in a way that brings glory to God. When I saw this and let go of my biases, I began enjoying my life in Mexico.

BECOMING A MOTHER

Let's rewind a bit. Not long after Andrew and I started dating, things were looking serious. On one of his visits to the eastern North Carolina town I lived in (six hours away from where he lived), I took him to my favorite bakery and sat him down. It was time for a heart-to-heart he had no idea was coming.

"I need you to know that I don't want biological children. I've wanted to adopt since I was little, and I don't plan on having my own kids. If that means we need to break up, that's okay," I said with my heart thumping. I braced myself for the scary unknown, because what I did know had sunk deep in my heart.

My desire to adopt was a mixture of my family history and my travels abroad. My maternal Italian-American grandmother and her second child died in childbirth before my mother turned two. My mother and her father moved into her aunt and uncle's house. During her childhood, my mom moved around some, but she mostly lived with them, so they were like parents to her. So I grew up calling my great-aunt Gina my grandmother and having two grandfathers on my mother's side. (I'm named after Gina.) My mother often talked about adoption and greatly admiring Dave Thomas (no relation to my husband), owner of the Wendy's fast-food chain. Every time we ate at a Wendy's when they had flyers on foster care, my mom brought a flyer home and talked about all that his foundation was doing to raise awareness and support for children in foster care.

So I let Andrew know that this was not a fleeting desire for me. He paused, put his pastry on his plate, and said, "I can see why you want to adopt. Would you consider having one child biologically and adopting others?" So the plan was laid out that day. Although I had no desire to grow my own baby bump, I made an oath to my soon-to-be husband.

About three years later, on a typical hundred-degree summer day in northern Mexico, I read the Old Testament passage about the Shunammite woman and Elisha.

> Gehazi answered, "Well, she has no son, and her husband is old." He said, "Call her." And when he had called her, she stood in the doorway. And he said, "At this season, about this time next year, you shall embrace a son." And she said, "No, my lord, O man of God; do not lie to your servant." But the woman conceived, and she bore a son about that time the following spring, as Elisha had said to her. (2 Kings 4:14-17 ESV)

My husband wasn't old, and I didn't have children because I chose to use birth control. Nonetheless I felt my spirit urging me to meditate on this passage. Meditation was the first step in a rather rapid process of God changing my heart from obligation to joy in having a child biologically. Cade was born fourteen months later. His middle name, Eliseo—the Spanish version of Elisha—came from this passage in the Bible, a constant reminder that God changes hearts.

When my Mexican neighbors and fellow churchgoers saw me pregnant, they asked me when the date was. They were *not* asking, "When is the estimated due date of your baby?" like Americans ask. Rather they were asking, "When is your scheduled C-section date for your baby?" I heard pregnant women saying things like, "I asked my doctor to schedule me on June 5, because that is my mother's birth date."[10] I was sure I would have a natural birth, and Andrew and I practiced the Bradley Method of breathing. I read all the books I could get my hands on. We wanted to do this as naturally as possible.

As I wrote in my book *A Smoldering Wick,*

On a hot day in August 2011, Cade was born by C-section. My water broke around 2 a.m., and when the contractions still hadn't started at 9 a.m., I went to see my doctor in Monterrey. Around 1 p.m., I was induced, and by 11 p.m., Cade wasn't budging out of his cocoon. His head was too big, and my hips—amazingly— were too small. So a C-section was performed, and at 11:37 p.m., I met my nine-pound (four-kilo) bundle of joy.[11]

Because of their job schedules, my extended family was with Cade only for a few days before they boarded a plane back to the States. I had no idea the struggle I was about to face as a new mother of a boy who was likely lactose intolerant for the first four months of his life. Breastfeeding was a major challenge, and it hurt so much at first. With the crib right next to our bed, I was able to pick up Cade immediately when he started his hungry cry every three hours. Andrew would wake up and rub my feet to help ease the pain. Sometimes he'd fall asleep at the foot of the bed.

Like most new parents, we were constantly tired. Recovering from a C-section, taking care of a new life, and being so far from family felt beyond overwhelming at times. Additionally, for the first four months, Cade cried for hours at a time. All science seemed to give me for this phenomenon was the word *colic.* I had no idea babies smiled before five months, because the colic didn't subside until I began introducing solid foods. (Four years later, after seeing some similar feeding struggles with our daughter, I quit eating dairy, and her colic disappeared within a week.)

I spoke Spanish with Cade from the beginning, and Andrew spoke English with him. We had heard this is one of the better ways for children to learn two languages, and it was relatively easy for us to do in Mexico. I was speaking Spanish a lot with nearly everyone around me, so speaking it with him came more naturally than I thought it would. At sixteen months old, *ball* was his first word. While most of the other kids his age were using several words, his language skills took time, something we knew to expect as his brain was working overtime in two languages. By the time we moved back to the United States when he was twenty-eight months old, he spoke mostly Spanish and had a hard time understanding his English-speaking grandparents.

Overall I'm grateful that I got to learn how to be a mom in a culture different from my own. I'm grateful for the way living in a relationship-centered culture taught me how to be a mother outside my own culture. I stuck with breastfeeding mostly out of economic necessity rather than a natural slant toward motherhood; but the research that pointed to "breastfeeding is better" didn't prepare me for months of colic.

I learned to give up my judgment of mothers who feed their babies formula, as more of my Mexican neighbors used formula than I'd expected. I learned that every other mom in the world, regardless of culture, had an opinion on how to mother best: "Put socks on his feet even if it is hundred-degree weather!" or "You can't give him cow's milk until he's at least twelve months old!" Even though I had given Cade life, he matured me at a rapidly increasing rate. His colic taught me to appreciate any and every smile, and it likely prepared me for mothering the four other children who came after him.

Life slowed way down for this type-A producer. And it wasn't easy. I needed to slow down to stay present with Cade, to play at his level, read at his level, sleep on his schedule. When I could find extra pesos in our budget, I was excited to purchase him a cheap toy from the toy stand at the market, even though I knew it was poorly made and wouldn't last long. Andrew and I bought few of his clothes. And the longing to provide not just necessities but also enjoyments was strong. Even when I was around women who breastfed openly, I still wanted (and used) a cover, not because of culture but because of me. When Cade hurt, I ached; when he slept, I either slept with him or was in hyperproductive mode, cleaning the house or working on my grad-school studies. I learned to make fresh baby food from our market bounty and started making homemade popsicles we could enjoy together. We'd watch *Hey Arnold!* together on Netflix nearly every day. He was my buddy and my baby. In many ways, our bond was stronger because of our circumstances. As he grew visibly, so I grew inside. We matured each other.

ON BEING AN IMMIGRANT MOTHER

A few months before Cade was born, Andrew and I were working on getting our FM3s, an immigration status in Mexico that included religious workers. It was a frustrating paperwork process that introduced us on a minor scale to the challenges of living as legal immigrants. We had been living on tourist visas until then. Those visas expired every six months, which meant we had to travel back to Laredo, Texas, cross the border, and sleep in the United States for one night then cross back into Mexico the following day. Our Mexican pastor was willing to vouch for our FM3s as religious workers.

The drug cartels traveled the road between Laredo and Monterrey a lot, and all of our Mexican friends advised us to get religious-worker visas, even just to decrease our travel. However, the timing of our FM3s posed a problem for our hoped-for trip back to the United States when Cade was a few months old.

In the hospital, we were given Cade's Certificado de Nacimiento, which needed to be taken to our municipality's Registro Civil office within ninety days. There they walked us through the process of getting Cade's official Mexican birth certificate. But there was an error on the hospital's certificate, so the Registro Civil wouldn't even look at it until we got the error corrected. A few days later, we returned to the municipal office with the corrected version. The administrator began asking us questions and filling out the official paperwork. When it came time to write down our son's last name, cultural norms slapped us in the face.

"What is his first last name?"

"Thomas," I answered.

"What is his second last name?"

"He has none."

"He has to have one."

"No, he doesn't. He's American. In the States, we only give one last name."

"But he was born in Mexico. In Mexico, we give two last names."

"I understand that, but he's born to American parents in Mexico."

"It doesn't matter. I won't fill out the paperwork unless you give me a second last name."

"Can't you just leave it blank?" I asked. We had prayed, searched, and anguished over the right name for the beautiful baby I held in my arms.

"No. You must give us a second last name. What is your last name?"

"Thomas."

"You both have the last name Thomas?" the administrator asked us, surprised.

"Yes, when we got married, I took Andrew's last name."

"Then we will put Thomas Thomas."

"No! His name is not going to be Cademon Thomas Thomas," I said fervently.

Andrew and I knew we needed to get this document as soon as possible, because the next step was getting the Consular Birth Abroad Report from the US consulate in Monterrey. We needed all of those documents to present to immigration in order to get our FM3s in addition to Cade's passport for our trip home.

We went home to discuss. The next day we were back, adding my maiden name to Cade's Mexican birth certificate. Cademon Thomas Smith. I'm not sure his white American identity could be any clearer.

But now there was another problem. We needed our FM3s issued before the administrator would put "religious worker" to describe our occupation on Cade's birth certificate.

We felt we were locked in a government game of keep-away. We were in the middle between those guarding Cade's Mexican birth certificate, those guarding our religious-worker visas, and those guarding Cade's passport. So we were visiting government offices often.

The immigration office was on the south side of Monterrey, about an hour from our house. They were open only from 9 a.m. to 1 p.m., three days a week, and if we hit too much traffic (which often happened in Monterrey) and the immigration lines were long, we wouldn't be seen and had to try another day.

I sent a prayer plea to our supporters:

Please pray that the Mexican government reviews our applications and everything is in order for them to give us the FM3 documents we need to then give to the local government to get Cade's birth certificate. Once we have the birth certificate we can go to the Consulate and send away for Cade's passport, but that will take 7-10 days to get to us . . . hopefully before our trip home on October 4.

Things were looking grim until one day at immigration when we happened to mention that we already had our plane tickets. The woman looked at us and asked if we had a confirmation email of the tickets. We did. It was like we had found the golden ticket from Willy Wonka's chocolate factory, and the immigration process sped up amazingly.

Unknown to us, our trip home would allow us to attend the funeral of my grandfather—that is, my great-uncle who I knew as my grandfather. I was grateful for this opportunity, because living so far from home had already kept us from my other Italian grandfather's funeral and two close friends' weddings.

Also, unbeknown to us, the government keep-away game prepped us for life with Julia, teaching us to stay on our toes, deal with a pending immigration status, and fill out every form meticulously.

ATTEMPTING ADOPTION

When Cade was about six months old, I began looking into the other side of our marital compromise: adoption. Based on the research I had done, it was necessary to find a placement agency accredited and approved in both the United States and in Mexico.[12]

On April 1, 2008, the United States entered into enforcement of the Hague Adoption Convention, which "aims to prevent the abduction, sale of, or trafficking in children, and it works to ensure that intercountry adoptions are in the best interests of the children."[13] Adoptions are temporarily shut down when a state commits to this convention "in order to make [the country's] programs compliant with Hague requirements before processing any more adoptions."[14]

We had been in Mexico for two and half years by the time Cade was six months old, and we were planning to be there for only a few more. After months of research and reaching out, I was left with several shut doors from Mexican placement agencies that didn't place with non-Mexican families and a few American-based agencies that didn't place with Americans who weren't living on American soil. At the end of the list was the one agency in our region that I was told placed some children with Americans living in Mexico. So I called.

"What requirements do you have for the families you place with?" I asked.

"Couples have to be married for three years," the woman said.

My mind said, *Check!* My heart said hope was possible.

"Parents must be at least eighteen and no more than forty-five years older than the child," she said.

Check! Hope.

"If there are biological children, the youngest must be at least six years old."

Door closed.

It was the final door I knew of, and I was frustrated, angry, and exhausted.

A few months later, when Cade was nine months old, I signed up for graduate school. Although I kept my ears perked for adoption potentials, my constant pursuit of the adoption dream was done. I needed to focus on the child I had been given and all the ways he taught me about being a better mom.

A few months after Cade turned two, our plans to return to the United States were coming to fruition. A month before the new missionaries were coming to Mexico, one of my high school English students confessed that she was pregnant with her boyfriend's baby. The grapevine brought word to me, and my heart jumped. She was sixteen, and her mom suggested adoption.

I phoned the consulate and the State Department, and we considered delaying our move by months, if necessary. A week later, the student confessed to lying about being pregnant.

I was emotionally low, but my heart was not as broken as I thought it would be. I had been studying for my master's in international development, and my perception of adoption had begun to change. Going through the program helped me realize that a lot of my desire to adopt was based on my savior complex.

Jayakumar Christian's book *God of the Empty-Handed* was required reading for my degree. Christian borrowed the term *god complex* from Jürgen Moltmann, who defined it as "humans and powers seeking to become gods."[15] Christian explains it this way:

> The relative powers within poverty situations play gods over the
> poor, creating god-complexes within poverty relationships. . . .

To sum up, god-complexes are 1. Clusters of power (social, economic, bureaucratic, political, and religious) within the domain of poverty relationships that absolutize themselves to keep the poor powerless; 2. A function of structures, systems, people, and the spiritual interiority within each cluster of power.[16]

Author Ryan Kuja explains a white savior complex this way: "The nagging sense of purposelessness that commonly haunts us is given the analgesic of an opportunity to rescue, to save—and thus to matter. It makes us feel better about who we are."[17] I'm still recovering from my white savior complex. Till the day I die, I believe I will need friends to call out this tendency of mine: a desire to fix others' problems with my resources and my privilege, creating a counterfeit sense of worth. Missionaries and social justice advocates are especially prone to this, and I've seen it in many others outside those arenas. The difference between being a friend to those who are marginalized and acting out of a white savior complex is subtle, so how we do justice work and missions work is critical. Walking alongside others is different from walking up to them and telling them how they should fix their problems or how they should let us fix their problems.

For the first time, I started seriously considering domestic adoption. All those closed doors to our potential adoption in Mexico may have been open doors for Mexican families. What once offended and frustrated seemed more nuanced and wise.

In December 2013, the Thomas family of three moved back to the United States much more mature, with little regret, and with no clue what the future would hold.

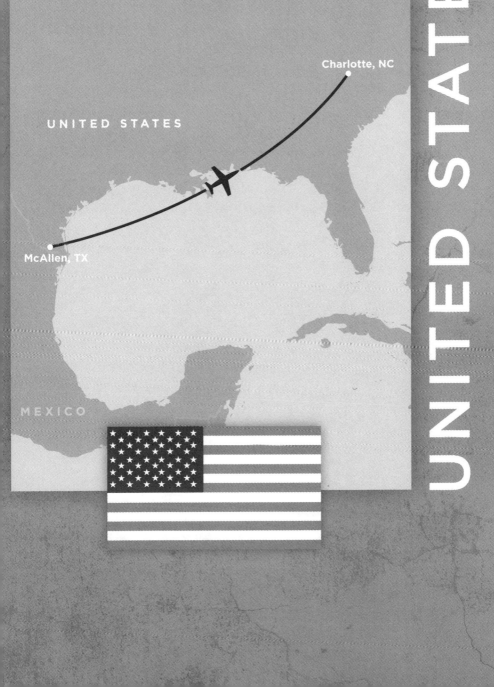

PART 3

UNITED STATES

Charlotte, NC

UNITED STATES

McAllen, TX

MEXICO

Chapter Five

UNACCOMPANIED MINOR

JULIA: 2018

n 2017, 36,616 unaccompanied minors crossed into the United States. Of them, 31,394 were apprehended, with the remaining 5,222 labeled as inadmissible, meaning they were unable to enter the country.[1] It seems that Julia could have been unaccompanied minor number 27,328 among those who entered the United States. But it's complicated, because Julia entered with her "stepfather."

In 2017, 76,457 family units crossed into the United States, 50,753 were arrested, and the remaining 25,704 were deemed inadmissible.[2] Julia could have been part of the 42,633rd family unit to enter the United States. But it's complicated, because Julia's stepfather didn't officially enter. He was deported.

Between October 2017 and April 2018, more than seven hundred children were separated from their parents at the border, including one hundred under the age of four.[3] Julia could have been the 101st child separated from her parental guardian. But Customs and Border Protection may not have categorized this as a separation, because Carlos didn't have papers stating he was married to Lupe. Or Carlos didn't pass a DNA test. Or CBP assumed he was trafficking Julia and separated them in an attempt to protect her.

So it's unclear which statistical category Julia falls under. After traveling up from Honduras and then through Guatemala, then in the cargo section of a tractor-trailer until the latter portion of Mexico, fainting three times, being separated from her mother, who was held

hostage by the smugglers who charged her family thousands of dollars
to cross, and then CBP deciding to deport Carlos, five-year-old Julia
officially became an unaccompanied minor in November 2017.

So, yes, she's one of the statistics. But no human is ever merely
a number.

JULIA SEPARATED FROM CARLOS
BY THE US GOVERNMENT

Julia doesn't remember what happened between the moment she left
her mom's side and the moment she went into US Customs and
Border Protection custody. Science points to something called dissociative amnesia, otherwise referred to as functional amnesia or psy-
chogenic amnesia, which is "a condition in which a person cannot
remember important information about his or her life.... Dissociative
amnesia has been linked to overwhelming stress, which may be caused
by traumatic events such as war, abuse, accidents, or disasters. The
person may have suffered the trauma or just witnessed it."[4]

Psychologist Dylan Gee, who studies how trauma and stress affect
the development of children, wrote an honest and disturbing article
in *Vox* after the 2,654 children were forcibly separated because of the
Trump administration's inhumane zero-tolerance policy. "The trauma
could change their brains forever," he said.

In many cases, the trauma of being separated from their parents
could be one in a long line of stressful experiences for a migrant
child. Many families seeking asylum are already fleeing danger,
and many children have already endured a harrowing journey
upon arriving at the border. Exposure to multiple traumatic
events places these children at even greater risk for mental
health disorders.[5]

In late 2018, I was able to take a trip to the Texas border with the
National Immigration Forum. While there, we visited Catholic Charities

of Rio Grande Valley's relief house. I spoke with Rita, who had come from El Salvador with her seventeen-year-old daughter and six-year-old son. She traveled with a group of migrants up through Mexico, but she said she didn't pay a smuggler. "We ran through the desert and hid behind cacti," she said. "There were dead bodies out there."

Border Patrol found Rita and her children and placed them in a holding cell that she and other immigrants call the *hielera*—the icebox—a nickname given to the facility because of how cold CBP keeps it. The temperature is a constant source of tension and litigation between the US government and immigration advocacy groups. The facilities are shared by two distinct groups with very distinct needs: Customs and Border Protection Officers (including Border Patrol Agents), who wear heavy, long-sleeve uniforms and are active in their jobs, and migrants, who have little clothing and are allowed little movement within the facility.[6] Disposable plastic Mylar blankets that look like long sheets of tinfoil are given for warmth.

After the *hielera*, Rita was taken to the processing center, or what migrants call the *perrera*—the dog pound.

Carlos and Julia were also caught by Border Patrol, placed in a *hielera*, and likely taken to Ursula processing center in McAllen, Texas (based on where they crossed over), which opened in 2014. In 2018, it served as the epicenter for zero-tolerance family separations.

The two were taken by bus to Ursula, where their personal items were taken from them, including their shoelaces to prevent suicide. The sorting process then began.

Likely within hours at the processing center, Julia moved from being with Carlos in the fathers-with-children caged section in the front of the warehouse to the UAC (unaccompanied alien[7] children) caged section in the back.

When Julia had to go to the bathroom, she had to ask to leave her cage and enter another: the female toilet cage. Depending on the cleaning schedule, it had between four and ten portable royal-blue toilets lined up in a row. They looked as though someone had sawed off the top of a typical enclosed toilet and the bottom of the toilet's door to help prevent sexual assault. Above the toilets hung ten foil ducts that matched the chainlink fences and the Mylar blankets. When Julia was done, she could return to the female UAC cage, lie down on her thin, army-green foam mat, and cover up with her foil blanket. She left the cage only to eat and to go to the bathroom.

It's unclear how long she stayed at Ursula, but the goal, Border Patrol agents told me, was to keep people no longer than seventy-two hours. For unaccompanied minors, that goal was usually met as they were then taken out of the US Department of Homeland Security agency and placed into one of the Department of Health and Human Services's agencies, the Office of Refugee Resettlement.

Lupe found out from Carlos's family that he was held at the processing center for two days. She had heard that the process typically take weeks, though I later found out it varies due to the many divergent paths a migrant may take. Much of what is done is based on the CBP Officer's autonomous decision-making.

Lupe heard from Carlos's family that he was back in Honduras but that "his mind isn't right."[8] She has tried to contact him but has not

THE BRIEF HISTORY

The Border Patrol began in 1924 in the Rio Grande Valley and was in charge of 316 border miles. Year-to-date in August 2018, there had been 148,000 apprehensions. Smuggling fees alone brought in $72 million a year to the drug cartels.[9]

In the fifty-five thousand square feet of the facility dedicated to families and unaccompanied minors, detainees were sorted based on age, gender, and family status into what the Border Patrol called four pods: one for girls seventeen and under, another for boys seventeen and under, mothers with children, and fathers with children.[10]

been able to. She and I both doubt that our many questions about what happened during his time under CBP watch will ever be answered. According to the US Customs and Border Protection website,

> An officer is responsible for determining the nationality and identity of each applicant for admission and for preventing the entry of ineligible aliens, including criminals, terrorists, and drug traffickers, among others. US citizens are automatically admitted upon verification of citizenship; aliens are questioned and their documents are examined to determine admissibility based on the requirements of the US immigration law.
>
> Under the authority granted by the Immigration and Nationality Act (INA), as amended, a CBP officer may question, under oath, any person coming into the United States to determine his or her admissibility. In addition, an inspector has authority to search without warrant the person and effects of any person seeking admission, when there is reason to believe that grounds of exclusion exist which would be disclosed by such search.[11]

Questions abound: Why have CBP officers taken on roles that only trained social workers should have? As my friend and author Sarah Quezada said, "There are no social workers in this processing center. We are addressing a humanitarian crisis with a national security response."

Typically the deportation process starts with the individual being arrested. If the arrest takes place within one hundred miles of the US border, and the individual has been in the United States for less than two weeks, an expedited removal is allowed.[12] In my research, I couldn't find out how long expedited removal typically takes, although I did find an article by a law office that said an individual who is to be expedited "will have to wait at the airport in the Secondary Inspection office until [his or her] next available flight, which could be 24 to 36 hours later."[13]

Criticism of expedited removals abound. According to the American Immigration Council,

> One of the major problems with expedited removal is that the immigration officer making the decision virtually has unchecked authority. Individuals subject to expedited removal rarely see the inside of a courtroom because they are not afforded a regular immigration court hearing before a judge. In essence, the immigration officer serves both as prosecutor and judge. Further, given the speed at which the process takes place, there is rarely an opportunity to collect evidence or consult with an attorney, family member, or friend before the decision is made.[14]

If an expedited removal doesn't happen, the traditional immigration court process begins. The individual receives a notice to appear in court (at least ten days prior to the court date) for removal proceedings; the notice lists the reasons the government believes the individual should be deported.[15] If removal is ordered at this point, the individual is usually detained in an immigration detention center or a privately operated jail contracted out by the federal government. The bond hearing is then set, where the judge determines the amount of the individual's bond "based on criteria such as an individual's local family ties, ability to post the bond, time in the United States, criminal record and how they entered the country," according to the American Immigration Council.[16]

Then a master calendar hearing is done by a federal immigration judge, a merits hearing, and then—unless the merits hearing ends with the judge allowing the individual to remain in the United States—there is an order of removal, which can be appealed. According to the American Immigration Council, "These appeals can take months and individuals can remain incarcerated during the appeal process, even those eligible for bond. . . . Individuals from Mexico are usually flown to US border cities and either walk or are bused across the border. Those from Central American countries are flown direct" by ICE Air Operation.[17]

Julia was processed as an unaccompanied minor while Carlos was deported. Social workers and legal counsel I spoke with found their separation confusing. Then I read a *New York Times* article that said, "New data reviewed by The New York Times shows that more than 700 children have been taken from adults claiming to be their parents since October."[18] I found out much later that US Customs and Border Protection since 2005 has been systemically separating children from their parents as a method of deterrence in what the Department of Health and Human Services calls a "consequence delivery system."[19]

When I read the *New York Times* article on April 21, the day after it was published, I didn't know that the zero-tolerance policy of separating children and parents at the border was already in effect. By the time I finished reading the article, I wept to the point of falling to the floor. Not knowing about DNA testing or the discrepancies between the US government's and the Honduran government's views of stepdad status, I believed Julia to be among the seven hundred separated children.

Like most of the general public, I didn't hear about the zero-tolerance policy until two weeks later, on May 7, when Attorney General Jeff Sessions announced the change in a gathering of Association of State Criminal Investigative Agencies.[20] However, it was quietly announced on April 6, published on the Department of Justice's website:

> Attorney General Jeff Sessions today notified all US Attorney's Offices along the Southwest Border of a new "zero-tolerance policy" for offenses under 8 USC. § 1325(a), which prohibits both attempted illegal entry and illegal entry into the United States by an alien. The implementation of the Attorney General's zero-tolerance policy comes as the Department of Homeland Security reported a 203 percent increase in illegal

border crossings from March 2017 to March 2018, and a 37 percent increase from February 2018 to March 2018—the largest month-to-month increase since 2011. Attorney General Jeff Sessions said,

> The situation at our Southwest Border is unacceptable. Congress has failed to pass effective legislation that serves the national interest—that closes dangerous loopholes and fully funds a wall along our southern border. As a result, a crisis has erupted at our Southwest Border that necessitates an escalated effort to prosecute those who choose to illegally cross our border.
>
> To those who wish to challenge the Trump Administration's commitment to public safety, national security, and the rule of law, I warn you: illegally entering this country will not be rewarded, but will instead be met with the full prosecutorial powers of the Department of Justice. To the Department's prosecutors, I urge you: promoting and enforcing the rule of law is vital to protecting a nation, its borders, and its citizens. You play a critical part in fulfilling these goals, and I thank you for your continued efforts in seeing to it that our laws—and as a result, our nation—are respected.[21]

When I read Sessions's announcement, again I collapsed in grief. The sobs wouldn't stop. As story after story came in of separation after separation—a mother from her eighteen-month-old, a father from his four-year-old, parents from their three children—the floor near my computer desk became the holy ground of my lament. It wasn't just Lupe going through this, but many others. More than three thousand parents did not know when or if they would see their children again.

CHILDREN CROSSING

Some coyotes charge less when children are involved, with the understanding that groups with children will be delivered to CBP officers. It's unlikely that the $7,500 Lupe and Carlos paid for transport from Honduras to the US border included evading Border Patrol. Typically, if coyotes successfully lead their customers past Border Patrol agents, more payment is required, even if it wasn't stated before.

In the book *Enrique's Journey* by Sonia Nazario, which I began reading one week prior to Julia becoming my foster daughter, Honduran teenager Enrique makes it past Laredo, Texas, with a coyote but has to get out of the Blazer he's riding in half a mile south of the Border Patrol checkpoint.

Enrique and the two Mexicans, with [coyote] El Tiríndaro leading, climb a wire fence and walk east, away from the freeway. Then they turn north, parallel to it. Enrique can see the checkpoint at a distance.

Every car must stop. "U.S. citizens?" agents ask. Often, they check for documents.

Enrique and his group walk ten minutes more, then turn west, back toward the freeway. They crouch next to a billboard. Overhead, the stars are receding, and he can see the first light of dawn.

The Blazer pulls up. Enrique sinks back into the pillows. He thinks: I have crossed the last big hurdle. Suddenly he is overwhelmed. Never has he felt so happy. He stares at the ceiling and drifts into a deep, blissful sleep.

Four hundred miles later, the Blazer pulls into a gas station on the outskirts of Dallas. Enrique awakens. El Tiríndaro is gone. He has left without saying good-bye. From conversations in Mexico, Enrique knows that El Tiríndaro gets $100 a client. Enrique's mother, Lourdes, has promised $1,200. The driver is the boss; he gets most of the money.[22]

Enrique's mother, Lourdes, was contacted not long after his arrival in Dallas. The fee increased to $1,700.

This is like many migrants' stories. For those processed through US Customs and Border Protection, the story looks different, but still coyotes and Border Patrol similarly lord over the children.

In 2015, the *Atlantic* interviewed a teenage El Salvadorean boy who told how he was processed through immigration in 2014. The first eight months of 2014 saw a 90 percent increase in the influx of unaccompanied minors, prompting then President Obama to involve the Federal Emergency Management Administration (FEMA), calling it an urgent humanitarian crisis.[23] Though the *Atlantic* used the boy's first name, I have chosen to omit it.

> [He] remembers a concrete floor in the hielera and so many kids crammed into the cell that they slept in shifts. They shared one toilet, and the water that agents provided tasted as if it was mixed with salt. "I didn't drink water for three or four days," [he] claimed.
>
> His experience with Border Patrol bore a similar haste and confusion to his time with the coyotes. At sundown one day, agents loaded him and other children onto a bus and drove them to an airport where [he] rode his first-ever airplane. When he landed he saw a large sign that read "Tucson, Arizona." Next, they stayed at a warehouse with rows of chain-link cages like indoor dog kennels. This was most likely an emergency shelter in Nogales, Arizona. Children here slept on pads with blankets seemingly made of tinfoil, beneath the omnipresent glow of fluorescent lights. The guards taught the kids American football. [He] said some placed bets on kids and made them race each other for microwavable burritos.
>
> . . . He [then] rode to Phoenix where he stayed in another shelter. Then two agents accompanied him and a few other children onto a plane at the airport bound for New York. There,

he lived in a comfortable shelter run by the Office of Refugee Resettlement. He called his mother daily, and after a few weeks, in mid-August, she drove from Virginia to pick him up.[24]

In Julia's case, her mother was not there to pick her up from the Office of Refugee Resettlement. Her sponsorship family was.

LIVING WITH THE SPONSORSHIP FAMILY

Marta, Carlos's sister, who was planning on welcoming Lupe, Carlos, and Julia, was contacted through the Office of Refugee Resettlement to be Julia's sponsor. It's unclear how this connection was made, but it was likely done through Carlos. But if CBP officers thought Carlos was trafficking Julia, why did they take his recommendation for who Julia could live with? The questions are innumerable.

Marta had been living in the States for a few years and had arrived through the same coyote Lupe had used. Marta crossed over the US border with her elementary-age daughter with no issues, and she had connected Lupe to her smuggler. After two plane rides to North Carolina, Julia arrived at her new home with Marta in November 2017.

Sponsorship families can be documented or undocumented. They are an important piece of the Trafficking Victims Protection Reauthorization Act of 2008, which says that "unaccompanied alien children (UAC) must be promptly placed in the least restrictive setting that is in the best interest of the child."[25] According to the Office of Refugee Resettlement's website, case managers are required to assess "the child's past and present family relationships and relationships to non-related potential sponsors." They are also required to interview sponsors, have them complete an authorization for release of information, conduct background checks, coordinate fingerprint checks, and, at times, coordinate a check of the immigration Central Index System.[26]

Thirty days after a child is placed in a sponsorship home, the Office of Refugee Resettlement (ORR) calls the sponsorship home to check on the child. If no one answers, ORR's report lists the child as "unac-counted for." There are no other checks. According to a spokesperson for ORR: "Once an unaccompanied minor is placed with a sponsor, he or she ceases to be in the custody of the US government, and all HHS-provided subsistence—food, shelter, clothing, health care and education—ends at that point, and the child becomes the responsi-bility of his or her parent, guardian or sponsor."[27]

In late spring of 2018, articles published by major news organiza-tions about 1,475 migrant children being "lost" by the federal gov-ernment caused widespread concern. As it turned out, many of those ORR thirty-day processing calls were left unanswered, likely because of a new relationship between ORR and ICE (US Immigration and Customs Enforcement).

According to an article in *Quartz* on May 28, 2018,

There are four levels of sponsors, according to ORR policy, be-ginning with parents, then siblings and close relatives, then distant relatives or unrelated adults, and finally willing strangers or agencies. Potential sponsors, once identified, must apply for unification with the child and provide evidence of a relationship. If the applicant is approved, the child is released. The ORR tries not to hold kids extensively, and data from 2015 show that children spent an average of 34 days in custody before joining a sponsor. Once a child joins a sponsor, the ORR relinquishes responsibility—that's what has people up in arms now. The sponsorship agreement essentially leaves it up to the child and their sponsors to show up for further immigration proceedings.[28]

The Office of Refugee Resettlement hadn't previously required documentation checks on sponsorship families, which meant that if an unaccompanied minor had an undocumented relative or friend already living in the United States, like Julia and Marta, they lived with that person. However, according to a *New York Times* article, due to a memorandum of understanding (MOU) between ORR and ICE, "The refugee agency will begin to provide ICE with information, including names, fingerprints, addresses, and phone numbers, on children's parents or sponsors, as well as of other adults living within the same household, according to a copy of the agreement obtained by the *New York Times*."[29] The same article published in May 2018 said that the MOU was signed "recently," but I was unable to find an exact date. Undocumented immigrants, who are in constant fear of the federal government, had reason to fear even more.

Maybe this is why Marta locked Julia inside her house. Marta's two school-age children lived with her, along with her sister, Celia, and Celia's two school-age children. Julia wasn't yet old enough to attend school. So when the women went to work and the children went to school, Julia stayed home alone. "Stay here and don't get into trouble," Marta told Julia, deadbolting the front door on her way out. Every once in a while, Marta would leave Julia with her neighbor if she was available to babysit.[30]

For months, Julia was left alone during the day, and according to her, she was given no food within reach. She remembers being made fun of by the family she lived with, and the other children took her food sometimes at supper, leaving her with an empty plate. During this time, she had some communication with Lupe.

"Anytime we chatted over video, she would be crying," Lupe said. "I didn't know what to do. If I confronted Marta, she might treat her even worse."

One day Julia figured out how to unlock the door. She walked out and went to the house of Jessica, a neighbor. Jessica gave me, Gena, more insight into the situation. "I gave her food, and she begged me to let her live with me and my family. My daughter and her got along well. I knew if I let her stay with me we'd have problems with her [sponsorship] family," Jessica said. One day Jessica gave Julia a new shirt. The next day, she saw the shirt being worn by Marta's daughter. "They never bought her anything," she said. "I felt so bad for her."

Marta was infuriated with Julia's escape. She threatened Julia with a beating if she left again. But when Julia made her mind up, very little stopped her. She left the house again in late February and wandered the streets, looking for someone to watch her. When another neighbor called the police, Julia was taken into custody of the state.

Chapter Six

DEPENDENT CHILDREN

GENA AND FAMILY: 2015-2018

JUNIPER

When we returned to the United States after living in Mexico for more than four years, I began writing my first book, *A Smoldering Wick*, in which I questioned why I was so willing to adopt internationally but so unwilling to pay attention to the vulnerable children from my own country. My mother was adopted unofficially when she was about two years old in what we would now call a kinship adoption. Two of my cousins were adopted. The desire to adopt internationally started in my own family and then solidified while I was in my twenties, mostly from my travels around the world, visiting orphanages and interacting with street kids. Unaware of my own white savior complex and the power dynamics of skin color, I unabashedly loved the pictures of white families taking in brown children.

International adoption— especially transracial adoption—is complicated.[1] Opinions on it are polarized. I had to wrestle with why I loved those pictures and why I wanted to adopt internationally. I had to come face to face with my biases and colonial mindset that fed the white-savior complex within me. Facing my inherent biases and mindsets is an ongoing process.

About six months after we returned from Mexico, we signed up for foster-care classes through our county, feeling that this was the best route for us to move toward adoption while simultaneously better understanding the needs of vulnerable children within our own community. Nine weeks into our ten-week class, we found out little Juniper was growing inside me.

A few months before Juniper was to arrive, Andrew suddenly lost his job. Despite our family being on welfare, experiencing a poverty we'd never expected in America, Juniper's birth was a sign of new life, and her name reflects that.

We rejoiced when she entered the world. I tried for a vaginal birth after a C-section, but it didn't happen. I rejoiced that I got to try. We gave her a name from another biblical passage that spoke to us, Isaiah 55:13: "Instead of the thornbush will grow the juniper, and instead of briers the myrtle will grow."

Three years later, we were finally ready to jump back into fostering. We received our foster license in September 2017, and in mid-October we got an email about a potential placement: two girls younger than our oldest, which at the time was our only boundary line. We had talked about being placed with one child, but after I heard the girls' story, I convinced Andrew we should go for it.

That night, we were placed with five-year-old Karen and four-year-old Emma, both with features like Juniper's: alabaster skin and sandy-blond hair. Karen and Emma weren't siblings, but they had lived together their whole lives, as far as we knew.

Andrew and I had moved to another country after seven months of marriage; we'd raised support from the mission field when a job fell through; we'd learned how to parent in Mexico far, far away from our families; and we'd started a coffee-shop ministry while we lived on minimal monthly support. Even so, that first week of foster care was the longest week of our marriage.

HOLY CUSS WORDS

"Whatchya doing?" four-year-old Emma asked.

"I'm changing Juniper's diaper," I said.

"It stinks," Emma said.

"Yup."

"All shit stinks."

"Yup, you're right," I responded, intently focused on holding back my surprise and laughter.

This was one of the first conversations Emma and I had, and I've never been able to get it out of my head. Foster care is the holiest of shit I've ever experienced.

House rules were boiled down to two: be respectful and be obedient. But there were other boundaries needed: don't use a belt to hit each other, homework isn't optional, fruit comes before junk food. Time-out happened a lot.

Mealtime was tricky: teaching the girls how to eat and to use napkins, discovering what they liked to eat, and trying to figure out how to begin healthy eating habits when one girl was very picky about food.

Bath time was tricky: keeping private parts behind closed doors, not knowing if there was any abuse associated with such things, and trying to figure out the logistics of bathing four children. Usually I gave Emma and Juniper a bath together, then Karen got a shower. Then when all the girls were dressed, Cade took a shower. The whole ordeal started right after supper and ended right before bed.

Bedtime was tricky: sitting still to read a book, finding books that piqued their interest and that didn't reference mommies and daddies too much (for the sake of sadness), and brushing teeth thoroughly. So we had to ease into it. We taught them "Twinkle Twinkle Little Star" and the ABC song, which they wouldn't stop singing. Then it was time for prayers and goodnight kisses. During those first few weeks, we had to walk out of the room, close the door, and let them cry themselves to sleep, which I wasn't prepared for. The wailing was heart-breaking. Often it'd keep Cade and Juniper awake, because our home had little sound insulation between rooms. "Why are they crying so much?" Cade would ask. We would try to have him imagine how he would act if he had to leave our home suddenly by himself and enter a new home where all the rules were new and all the food was different.

Transportation was tricky: getting Karen to a school far from our home and picking all the kids up on time. This was impossible for one parent to do, which meant work hours suffered.

We were exhausted. Ex—haus—ted.

After one full week of the girls being in our home, we met Karen's dad and Emma's mom, dad, and grandma. I was nervous because of stories the girls had told me and stories I'd heard from the social workers. I'd wake up for my early-morning bike ride in the dark, and fear would come upon me. Did their family follow the social worker to our house? Were they lurking about in the dark? Would they come after us?

The meeting went fine, and the family seemed grateful that we were caring for the girls. It was clear that the girls missed their family like crazy. We'd heard stories of birth parents who show no emotion. But that was not their family. There were tears and wailing. And there were smiles, especially when Andrew found common ground with them.

"The girls love flitters," Emma's dad said.

"We'll make them for them!" Andrew responded.

"Do you know what they are?" Emma's dad asked doubtfully.

"Yes, they are flat pancakes. I grew up in the country."

The whole family laughed and smiled at him.

"They like to go fishing too," Emma's dad added.

"Okay! I got a spot," Andrew said. "I can take them to do that."

I didn't open up my mouth much during that meeting. I knew I'd get too emotional if I did. Andrew handled it like a champ, and we gained a rapport with them we hadn't expected. The fear of the unknown was like a giant scary shadow of a tiny mouse.

One of my good friends, Laurel Fiorelli, had recently opened her home to a refugee family. I emailed her about the new addition to our home. She responded,

> The first thing I thought when I read your email was "holy shit."
> Literally, that is some "holy" "shit" right there. . . . I can just

imagine you and Andrew, shoulders tense from hugging kids and hauling backpacks, foreheads in perpetual wrinkle from emotions of all sorts day in and day out, wanting to pray but being exhausted or forgetting or opting to spend time—I don't know—actually talking to each other instead. And it is the most beautiful thing I have imagined in a long time. . . . We've had ups and downs and are learning so much. Much of what you mentioned in your email resonated; this seems to be a time of life where we have our noses to the grindstone and God feels really far away. We've been hit with all sorts of mishaps, including no sleep and random things that sometimes just feel like salt in the wounds, like working hard to get our baby down for a nap only to have noise from the family wake him up, or unknowingly missing our daughter's school event because I overlooked the notice in the sea of emails that I'm never able to wade through fast enough. It's a whole other realm of worry and fear and my own guilt to work through day by day. And as you and I and our spouses waddle like idiots through this disastrous beauty, I can't help but wonder if God is smiling—wait, maybe laughing—at us?! I know he is faithful even when I can't feel it. I know he is loving even when I can't feel it. I know he is near even when I can't feel it. But I still want to feel it and not just know it. And that seems to be the tension these days, between the knowing and the feeling.

Laurel had described our lives better than I could. Having four kids was absolutely crazy for us. I felt pulled in many directions all day long. The logistics of getting everyone out of the house was maddening, and Emma wasn't yet in school. We had to find a preschool that took foster-care vouchers and had an opening, which limited our options. My work hours decreased, but I was grateful to have a flexible job that allowed me to take off the time I needed.

As soon as the kids got home from school, it was homework time, then dinnertime, then bath time, then reading time, then bedtime. Around nine, Andrew and I fell into our bed, barely able to hold a conversation with each other. Sex was infrequent, fighting was increasingly normal, and the emotional weight of it all felt unbearable. We began speaking to each other in Spanish in front of the children in order to have some adult conversation.

After one month of this and of physical altercations initiated by Karen, we asked for the social worker to find her another home. Feelings of guilt and shame bubbled up. Karen required one-on-one attention, as she was falling behind in school and needed someone to walk her through her homework step by step. That was impossible with the demands of the other kids.

Karen and I went on a walk around our neighborhood, and I asked, "What do you think about living in a home without Emma?"

"Good," she said smiling.

"You've had to protect her a lot, haven't you?" I asked.

"Yes. I needed to keep her safe."

"Do you think she's in a safe home now?"

"Yes," she said firmly.

"What do you think about not having to keep her safe anymore?"

"That would be nice."

"What do you think about living with the couple you met recently?"

"Yes!" she said excitedly. "Do they have a dog at their house? Do I get my own room?"

"Yes, they have dogs, and yes, you'll have your own room."

When the new foster parents came to pick Karen up, she said goodbyes quickly to each of us, including Emma, and then happily jumped in their car. Leading up to her move, I had talked with other foster parents who had gone through the same thing—especially her soon-to-be foster mom, who encouraged me not to feel shame. She'd had her own pain when having to transition previous foster placements.

But some of that guilt wasn't unfounded. In her article "5 Dos and Don'ts of Foster Parenting," Tammy Perlmutter expressed the lack of belonging felt by foster children. Every move to another foster home only deepens that lack of belonging. Perlmutter, who was placed in three foster homes and a children's home, wrote, "For myself, since family life was such an abject disaster, the city of Philadelphia became my home and my identity, my comfort and my sense of belonging. With no one close or consistent enough to imprint on, I imprinted on the city. Kids find familiar territory a relief from their uprootedness."[2]

Contributing to a child's uprootedness is not something we took lightly. We felt we were all falling apart, and we knew that would happen at first. But the rebuilding after falling apart didn't seem to be happening. How much time would be enough time?

These are the murky waters of foster care. How much sacrifice is more than bearable? How much of making it work is avoiding the fear of failure? How much of the child's needs should be met before we meet our own? What lines are we not willing to cross? How many emotional breakdowns do we allow our biological children to walk through before we say it's too much? I don't have the answers to these questions, and I'm not sure I trust anyone who says they do.

Growing up in evangelical spaces, I was taught to seek out the answers the Bible has to life's questions. Becoming a foster mom has shown me that the gospel often convicts us to get involved in the gray areas of life, with or without the answers. Sometimes we seek answers when we simply need to seek relationships. The Bible doesn't always have the answers to life's questions. The Bible pushes me to a position of asking questions I never imagined I should ask. In an odd way, getting over the discomfort of asking the tough questions brought me closer to the gospel of Christ. He posed questions often, and in his parables, he left the answers unspoken.

A LAMENT FOR FOSTER CHILDREN

The day Karen left our home, I wanted to grasp for order beyond the chaos of fostering. In his book *Prophetic Lament*, Soong-Chan Rah wrote, "In the midst of this chaos, some sort of spiritual order is sought. . . . We need to know that there is order beyond our present reality."[3] Even though Karen was excited about her new home, I knew that honeymoon would end, and I had to hold onto hope that when it did, she would be able to find order piece by piece beyond the transition.

Rah informs his readers of a lament tool in the form of an acrostic. He shows the pattern found in the book of Lamentations, where the author uses the Hebrew alphabet as a way to guide the lamentations and to find fullness, shape, and form in them.

I wrote the following lament in acrostic form. As I wrote, I felt guilt, I felt shame, but I also felt hope that the next home would give Karen things ours couldn't.

Today marks a culmination of decisions that have me, once again, feeling the heaviness of lament. So once again, I have turned to the acrostic. I am thankful for this tool in the midst of weighted pain.

I lament:

for the Adulting you had to do at such a young age.
for the Bonds that must get prematurely cut.
for the Control you should have over your life but don't.
for the Decisions made without your input.
for the Environment you had to grow up in.
for the 'Foster' put before your name, and the prejudice that
      will come from it.
for the Grotesque scenes you've witnessed.

for the Heaviness you carry with you.

for the Isolation you constantly feel.

for the Juxtaposing you do daily between your life and
    everyone else's.

for the Knowledge that has come to you out of its
    proper order.

for the Lying you've learned to mimic.

for the Mountains others will call molehills.

for the Notes home from teachers that wouldn't be there if . . .

for the Opportunities that never were.

for the Pains of growing up that are deeper than most kids
    your age.

for the Questions that may never be answered.

for the Rights that may terminate or may not terminate.

for the Songs of childhood you never learned to sing.

for the Tension you may always hold between your past and
    your future.

for the Unwillingness for most people to understand you.

for the Visions of horror and the visions of home you hold in
    your mind's eye.

for the Ways the people of God have not been intentional
    about loving you.

for the X-rays that show and don't show the abuse.

for the Youth that was stolen and will never fully return.

for the Zeniths of times with blood family that may all be in
    the past.

for this I pray.

for this I lament.

For the ways in which I have been selfish in my love for you, I
    lament, I repent.

Christ have mercy.[4]

INTERTWINED KINGDOMS

Life calmed down as far as interpersonal issues were concerned, but we still were in survival mode. We began finding a rhythm, though it was at a faster pace than we wished. Medical appointments, therapy appointments, and parent meetings were now a part of every week.

As we sat in the waiting room at one of Emma's appointments, she opened a magazine and pointed at a beautiful woman inside. "Is this you?" she asked. Earlier that day, she approvingly told me I was skinny though she didn't know I had been dieting. My heart melted.

But her warmth turned real cold, real quick. "Why are you touching me?" she asked as I tried to rub her back, even though she was leaning on me.

If you were to graph the ebb and flow of compassion and correction between Emma and me, it'd look as jagged as a barbed-wire fence. Bursts of correction followed every burst of negative behavior; between were random moments of empathy, compassion, and reception.

Emma had a way of pushing buttons I didn't even know I had. I'd thought that Cade and Juniper had pushed me to the limits of my love, but Emma pushed me even further. In those moments of stretching, the realizations were heavy and hard. But now I see how the stretching grafted new boundary lines, like a piece of material stretched hard that never returns to its original size.

In many ways, it feels like human love is supposed to be stretched like that, like the original fabric of our faith was always meant to expand. But growth comes only through the realizations of how depraved we are. Without understanding how ugly I can be, I can't grasp the robustness of gospel love. Gospel love is jagged, ugly, and messy more than it is dignified and smooth. But I think I'm finally understanding why.

The kingdom of darkness and the kingdom of heaven are enmeshed on this earth. They are two trees whose roots and branches have entangled with each other. The work of the gospel is delicately separating the kingdom of darkness from the kingdom of heaven within ourselves and within the world. The demon within me has never been so apparent as when I'm fighting the demons around me. So often in this world, when we approach one kingdom, we approach them both.

When we approached fostering, we were in one of those thin places of this world, where earth and heaven are closest—and gray clouds make everything foggy. Every time I've approached a thin place, I've also sensed a heaviness that the forces of darkness lay in wait as well. The jagged, ugly ways I learn to trust God as a foster parent have me on the brink of a precipice, one step away from entering either kingdom. Selfishness comes out when, in my introverted desires for silence, I roar at my children when they have stories to tell. Anger arises in me when my children refuse to do what I've asked, and I have to walk away so I don't do something that could revoke my license. Annoyance attacks when I have yet another message from a social worker I need to respond to, another doctor's appointment I need to take off work for, another in-service training to sign up for, another court date I should attend. There is a strong temptation to walk away from all of this without regard to how it would affect anyone else involved.

Yet it's clear that the justice I seek is hidden beneath the injustices I impose on others. The kingdom of God is a mirror reflecting the kingdom of darkness within me. I can't enter the looking glass without first recognizing who I really am. Fostering has shown me this more than any church service, more than any woke preacher, more than any charismatic experience.

The gospel is both terrible and terrific because I am the worst of sinners and a daughter of the good King *simultaneously*. The gospel is both terrific and terrible because my foster daughter is a hot mess and yet a beautiful princess *simultaneously*. The gospel is both terrific and terrible because my house is a mixture of a yelling pad and a safe house, and I often feel like the strictest of teachers with sporadic moments of a mother in love with her brand-new baby.

Fostering has brought me much confusion but one absolute: I see my sin more clearly than I ever have, but I see the kingdom of God more clearly too.[5]

Chapter Seven

FOSTER DAUGHTER

JULIA, GENA, AND FAMILY: 2018

GETTING TO KNOW JULIA

On the Saturday after we first received Julia, we had a family birthday party to attend. Lots of kids, cupcakes, doughnuts, and balloons. Overstimulation and excitement. Tree swings and trampoline jumps. Introductions to family members who couldn't pronounce her name correctly. She was happy, loving, and taking it all in.

When it was her turn to swing the piñata stick, my sister-in-law and I looked at each other and agreed: she was not four years old. About a week later, we got an actual birth date and found out she was five and a half. When Smarties and Twix candies came pouring out of the piñata, she showed off her knowledge of this familiar system by grabbing as much as she could as quickly as she could.

Monday came, but neither ICE nor ORR showed up in court. We were rescheduled for the following Monday, and Andrew was not surprised.

Four kids for one week? Okay, we can do this, I thought. We were back in survival mode. But this time the layers of complication felt endless: cultural differences, language issues, interpersonal interactions, along with deep needs for adult affirmation and attention from both of our foster daughters. Emma would come up to me and say, "My Gena." Juniper would follow suit. Julia would do the same. "I'm everyone's Gena," I said, annoyed, trying to assure them there was enough of me to go around. But I wasn't convinced of my own words, and my annoyance didn't go unnoticed.

When the four kids tried to talk to me or Andrew at the same time, we'd fire back in English and in Spanish. Often we'd speak the wrong language to the child conversing with us. We had to change some of our Mexican vocabulary to Honduran vocabulary, and when I didn't remember certain Honduran words, I'd send a quick message to Elí Romero for translation. We had to teach Julia rules of the home that we never had to teach Emma: toilet paper goes in the toilet, and only adults cook the food. We were used to the kids getting into tiffs, but those escalated sooner and deeper.

"Tell her that is my toy! I want to play with it," Emma said.

"*Es mío!*" said Julia.

Then Cade explained, "Well, what actually happened was that Julia had the toy and then Emma grabbed it and then Julia grabbed it back."

Not only were we translating as parents, we were translators between the children. We would have made millions as a reality TV show. The real reality was that it was wearing us down. We were tired mentally, emotionally, and physically.

The temper tantrums from Emma increased, and we felt we were moving backward with her. She and Julia could set each other off at any moment. Initially we trod lightly, afraid of the erupting volcanoes. Then we realized we had to be smart about letting them erupt in controlled environments.

Julia would shut down if she was corrected. Often she'd walk into her room, change into her favorite pajamas and flip-flops, pick up her large pink toy car along with the black tote bag the social workers had given her, and walk toward the back door. When we stopped her, she'd throw a temper tantrum. The streets were not foreign to her, and she seemed to think she could walk home to her mother.

I took off work because we didn't have anywhere for Julia to go during the day. I began looking for daycares that had openings, but I couldn't find any bilingual slots available. We had to be prepared if ORR and ICE didn't show up again.

On Friday, Julia started her first day at an all-English preschool. When we arrived at school that morning, she wouldn't get out of the car. The temper tantrums were pretty regular those first weeks, so I wasn't surprised. When I struggled to peel her fingers off the headrest she had curled them around, my body was tense and my blood boiling. I felt love, anger, sadness, frustration, and compassion toward her, her mom, her previous caregivers, DHHS, and the whole situation—all at once.

In time, Julia came to trust us, and that grew most apparent when we saw her distrust of others. A few months after she had come to live with us, we decided to take her out to eat at a Honduran restaurant. We knew of only one, which was about thirty minutes away. By the time everyone was home and ready to go that Friday night, it was seven o'clock. Andrew and I decided the thirty-minute drive was too much for hungry stomachs, and before we opted for our favorite Mexican restaurant about five minutes away, I did one final Google search on Honduran restaurants. It told me there was one ten blocks from our house. We decided to drive by, thinking there was a glitch in Google's omniscience. We knew there was a restaurant there, but we'd always thought it was Dominican, based on the adjacent businesses. We parked and walked up.

"My aunts work at a place that looks like this," Julia said. (She always called the adult women of her sponsorship family *tías*, meaning aunts.)

"Oh yeah?" I said, dismissing her thoughts quickly as I often did to unnecessary chatter when hangry (hungry + angry) stomachs were waiting.

As we walked in the door and told the waitress we needed a table, we put on our tough skin as we felt and saw the stares of everyone in the place. Immediately we heard something we didn't expect.

"*Hola*, Julia," said a rotund woman sitting right next to the door. She had interrupted her cellphone conversation to say hi.

We all turned around, and I tightened my grip on Julia's hand. I didn't know if this was Marta or Celia, but I felt a maternal urge to protect.

Julia was silent, and her countenance dropped in a way I'd never seen before. The bold, brave, resilient Julia I knew so well looked like she suddenly had much to be ashamed of.

"Hi, my name is Gena," I said.

"And I'm Andrew."

"So you have her now?" the woman asked.

"Yep."

"She's going to stay with you forever?" she asked.

"No, she's going to go home to her mom," I said.

She turned her gaze to Julia. "You aren't going to say hi to me? Come give me a hug."

Reluctantly Julia slowly let go of my hand and walked over to the woman, who hadn't yet introduced herself. I felt like a tiger ready to pounce if she made any sudden moves. Julia gave her a hug and quickly linked hands again with me.

The waitress said our table was ready. Relieved the interaction was over, we moved quicker than normal to the table several feet away. When we sat down, Julia told me that the woman was Marta's sister, Celia.

"Do I have to go live with her again?" Julia asked with fear in her eyes.

Trying hard not to cry, I said, "Absolutely not. You will live only in our house until you go home to your mom."

Julia's cheerful countenance returned, and she goofily drank her beloved Coke, a drink we rarely let her partake in, though she craved it a lot. A huge *baleada*—typical Honduran handmade tortilla with beans, eggs, avocado, and cheese in it—arrived to Julia's utter delight.

THE CONUNDRUM

Monday came, but no agency did. This was turning into a long-term placement. Leading up to that second court date, Andrew and I were struggling to figure out what we'd do if they didn't show again. We'd tried for a little while to see if we could manage four children. I probably held on longer than I should have, but I wanted to make it work. I was just starting to see some major breakthroughs with Emma, and I felt very attached to her.

After five months of being in our home, a lot of things had progressed impressively in Emma, including her speech and her academics. When she first came to us, she didn't know the alphabet. She wouldn't sit still to read even the shortest of books. She pronounced things so poorly, I often couldn't understand her English. And touch—nope, she wouldn't do that. No hugs, no kisses, little to no eye contact. And she wouldn't say hello or goodbye to anyone.

By the time Julia arrived, Emma knew the first letter of the name of everyone in the house, and she proudly spoke them at random intervals. She picked out two books before bedtime and whined if we didn't read a third. She was pronouncing things so well, there didn't seem to be a need for speech therapy. She'd run up to us, squeeze us, and ask us to put her "in our clutches"—a phrase Andrew said when he picked her up in his arms like a baby. "I've got you in my clutches," he'd say and then often proceed to tickle her.

Emma would kiss my cheek and ear often, giggling when it tickled me. There was lots of eye contact. She'd say hello and goodbye as if it were the easiest thing in the world.

But one thing didn't progress at all: her relationship with our son. They seemed to annoy each other a lot; they rarely played with each other; and when they did, it didn't take long for one or both to fall apart. The week before Julia came into our home, we talked with our social worker about our concern with the dynamics between Emma and Cade.

When Emma first came into our home, her social worker made us think her parents were doing everything they needed for her to return. We always thought she'd be reunified. When that social worker was fired, Emma's new worker told us a different story. Things were going slowly. Very slowly. By the time Julia arrived, there was no way to tell if Emma was on the road to reunification or not.

Nonetheless we had to make a decision. At the time of Julia's placement, no other foster families in our county had parents who spoke Spanish. In two families, a female adult spoke Spanish. From experience, we knew how tough it is when only one family member speaks the language and the other doesn't, and Julia had shown signs of major distrust with males. We also knew how tough it is to foster; the struggles of fostering would only heighten with language barriers involved.

We were in the epitome of a conundrum: what seemed best for one child conflicted with what seemed best for another. The social workers were willing to make an exception because of the language barriers, but normally one child was never moved so another could take her place. Our social worker could find other families who could meet Emma's needs, but she didn't want us to choose Julia because we felt obligated.

We had heard the statistics, so we knew a move would be a setback for Emma. According to an article in the *Atlantic*, "Students in foster care move schools at least once or twice a year, and by the time they age out of the system, over one third will have experienced five or more school moves. Children are estimated to lose four to six months of academic progress per move, which puts most foster care children years behind their peers."[1]

Emma's parents also needed to be considered. I felt connected to her mom as I prayed a lot for her and sent her pictures as often as I could. I would do my best to encourage her, reminding her of Emma's sweetness and that I was praying for her.

Yet with all we knew, and after what felt like walking through a deep emotional pit, we decided to move Emma.

Most foster parents feel guilt and shame when a child they foster moves to a different home. And this was the second time we had transitioned a foster child. So, for a second time, I had to battle feelings of guilt and shame.

But we also had to consider not only what's best for the foster child and for us as foster parents but also for our two biological children, whose best interests often clashed with the best interest of others involved. Additionally there was another foster child in our home whose language barrier prevented her from having many other options for placements.

Emma had been on a weekend of respite with another foster family—that is, with her new placement. Her new foster mom and I met to talk things over. I told her about Emma's favorite songs and books, her bedtime routine, and her tantrums. She told me how her own background was similar to Emma's. She had also grown up in a difficult home.

I told Emma the couple she'd been hanging out with wanted to have her in their home. She smiled and asked, "For a long time?" I said yes. Still smiling, she said nooo smugly, like she was being asked to do something mischievous and knew she shouldn't.

Emma's new foster mom felt a special connection to her, and she gloated over her. I dropped off Emma's things while she was at school so she could arrive at her new home and see her own clothes in the closet and her teddy bear, favorite stuffed rabbit, and princess blanket on her new bed. Her foster mom showed off her room, which had a new pink comforter and pink lamp that she had just bought. (Pink was Emma's favorite color.) She showed me Emma's bathing suits, which she'd bought for their upcoming beach trip, and the new flip-flops Emma had shown interest in when they went to the store together.

Her foster mom was bubbling with joy. I thought, *Every child deserves this excitement.* I don't remember ever bubbling with joy over Emma. Maybe it was the chaos of four children. Maybe we were in survival mode too often. I don't know, but I left very happy for the home this sweet girl was walking into. A home willing to adopt her if rights were terminated. A home where she'd get one-on-one attention, which would help prepare her for elementary school. A home with an adult that had lived in similar shoes. These were all benefits that our home couldn't offer her.

I was able to communicate with Emma's mother briefly about the transition. I've maintained communication with her.

I don't want to give the impression that transition isn't hard for foster children or that having a new foster mom with new stuff will solve transitional issues. I want to acknowledge that a foster child who has transitioned from one home to another may think it was a wrong decision. My evangelical upbringing taught me to ask questions like, What is God's will in situations like this? I once held beliefs like "God has one soulmate for everyone" and "you can miss your calling," but life has shown me otherwise: many decisions are made from a spectrum of possibilities rather than one good-versus-bad option.

In my brief experience with foster care and based on what I've heard from other foster parents, there's little black and white. So much of it is gray. Having biological kids in the mix seems to make it grayer. So much is unknown. So much is hoping and praying that we, the social workers, the parents, the child, and the courts make the right decision in whatever moment a decision needs to be made. And most decisions are complicated.

In her study "Voices of Foster Youths: Problems and Ideas for Change," Rita Morris shared the frustrations of the foster process according to youth who have lived it.

Another youth stated, "I was so tired of moving. I had moved over 30 times. I did not unpack my bags anymore because I would lose my things." . . . Many children were distressed by unexpected differences in rules both between and within foster homes. One said, "Sometimes it seems that every new house or every house place I went to had different rules. . . . I lived not knowing if what I was doing was right. I got to the point where I could fit no more."[2]

One month after Julia moved in, Emma moved out. They had lived in the same room, argued over the same toys, and fought equally for our attention. We were thankful for meeting Emma, for the ways we mutually grew together, for her willingness to love us and let us love her as best we all knew how. We were thankful we got to know her new foster parents. Thankful for the house full of love she was moving into. Thankful we would still see her in our foster-family meet-ups and future respites.

One day before Emma's move, Cade fell apart in our bedroom. He was doing his homework there because the house was full of family who had come to say goodbye to Emma. I found him lying on the floor, crying. "Everyone is ignoring me," he said through body-jerking sobs. I pulled him into my clutches, wrapping my arms around his skinny frame. Although his shyness worked against him in these big-group settings, I couldn't blame him for what was clearly true: we *had* been ignoring him. At six years old, he was the eldest in the family, and rarely did he request anything from us. He understood over and over again when we had to tend to the crying tantrums of his two-year-old sister or the kicking and screaming tantrums of his foster sisters. I'd probably told him, "Just a minute, buddy," a zillion times that month, only halfway hearing his stories and rarely asking him questions.

Many kids experience what Cade did, whether the circumstances surrounding the feelings of being ignored are due to foster care, parents who suffer extreme or subtle workaholism, parental substance abuse, distracted parents, and so on. Though this neglect happens in many families, its prominence in foster care has been documented. In a study of the needs of biological children who are a part of fostering families, feeling ignored was found to be a normal response of biological children.

Some children talked about "being ignored," "not getting that much attention," and "being alone," because the foster child became the center of attention in the home. The children thought that foster children were more visible to their parents, perhaps because of their challenging behaviors, and the children deemed that to be unfair. One child complained that their parent is always "doing everything for [the foster child] and not me."[3]

It was clear we had pushed our limits as a family, and we needed to step back and address everyone's needs. I had to grasp tightly to hope that God would guide Emma. Hope that her new placement would last as long as she needed a placement. Hope that she'd one day understand why she moved. Hope that we were a part of a loving foundation her life would be built upon.

Fostering is messy, and while I knew without a doubt that we didn't do everything right, I also knew that we couldn't be afraid of the mess if we were going to stay involved.

MEETING LUPE

Three weeks after being placed with Julia, we were introduced to her mom, Lupe, through a video chat. At the time, Lupe and Julia had been separated for nearly four months. During that chat, we ironed out details of the story that were completely wrong.

"Julia, *mi princesa, estás bien?* (Julia, my princess, are you okay?)" Lupe asked, holding back her emotions. (She did that for a full forty-five minutes, just as the social worker had asked her to.)

Julia was ecstatic. She took the phone around the house and showed her mom where she slept and introduced her to each of the inhabitants of the house, prancing like a princess, showing off her kingdom. "And, Mom, look at this big TV!" she said.

"Ooooh," Lupe responded with a smile.

Then I took my phone in my bedroom and closed the door. I sat on the carpet to the left of our queen-size bed. And Lupe let it out: weeping over her daughter, weeping about whether or not she'd ever get to hold Julia in her arms again, weeping over the awful details of her own journey that I had yet to hear about.

"If I came to the US border, would they give me my daughter back?" she asked. Looking back on that question, I stand amazed that she would even consider walking through hell again.

I tried to explain foster care to her, a framework that doesn't exist in Honduras. I told her to stay put, that we'd be working together to get them reunited.

Then we wept together. A lot.

I had never understood the heaviness of the word *desperate* before our conversation. She told me she hadn't been able to sleep well since they were separated. The next day, she said she'd slept well for the first time in months.

When the social worker first called us about Julia, in my ignorance of her history, I admit adoption was on my mind. I realized later that it was on theirs as well. But everything changed when we got Lupe's phone number in Honduras, and Julia got to video chat with her.

Though I had never experienced anything like her desperation, my heart yearned, and it had begun intertwining with hers.

Desperation, I thought, *wraps its arms around her uninvited. She falls apart and falls asleep in its cocoon. She will be made new. But not yet, not now. Now she feels as though she will die and turn to dust. She's not far from welcoming death, as earth is hell. There is an abyss separating her from her daughter, and she swears it will swallow her whole. Desperation is the shadow that follows her around.*

I had to grasp tightly to hope. Hope that God would guide Lupe. Hope that her will would remain strong in the midst of such heartache. Hope that she'd one day understand that Julia's move into our home was the first step in redirecting her back into her mother's arms. Hope that we'd be who we needed to be for both mother and daughter, for our own children, and for each other during this tough time.

Chapter Eight

"¿QUIÉN ES USTED A MÍ?" ("WHO ARE YOU TO ME?")

JULIA, GENA, AND FAMILY: 2018

When Julia came into our home, we were attending a racially diverse church. It was a true blessing for us because we'd struggled with the lack of intention surrounding racial justice in many white evangelical churches. Looking back, we know that God had us there for more than what we could see with our eyes. Pastor Antoine not only challenged us spiritually and gave us insight into being a black evangelical pastor after the 2016 election, he also had a background in foster care. In fact, that small church included several folks who intersected with foster care. Antoine, Sweet, and Chrissy had backgrounds in foster care, and Amanda was acting as a foster mom to the boy she took care of, though he wasn't in the system and she wasn't getting a stipend.

So when we showed up with Emma and Karen and then Julia, the community was beyond supportive. They asked the questions we didn't know we needed to be asking. "Are you taking advantage of respite care?" one former social worker asked us. "When she acts out, try to pinpoint the triggers. Is it because she's hungry? Is she overwhelmed by the social environment? Does it happen around the same time every day?"

Church wasn't an unfamiliar environment for Julia. In our video chats and text messages, Lupe spoke about God as much as I did. Sometimes we had deep theological discussions in our WhatsApp chat. "Why has God allowed me to go through this?" Lupe would ask.

I had no answers. All I could do was remind her that she was a strong woman, the strongest I had ever known, and that God knew her heart and loved her with all of his.

One day Lupe video-called us from a service at her Catholic church, because she wanted Julia to see some of the congregants from her home church and remind us that they were praying for us. They stood in a circle of white chairs, singing songs in their simple concrete building.

At the time we said goodbye to Lupe, who was sitting outside, the priest was preaching a sermon. I was grateful to know that she had a church community surrounding her.

Church community reminds us that we aren't alone and that we need people with us in the deep trenches of life. I was especially grateful for our church after several conversations with Julia about her skin color. "People of my skin color don't treat me well," she told me. When she moved into our home, she said, "I don't like my skin color." I was seriously concerned and wondered if our white family was the right fit. But as she interacted more with Katrina, her amazing African American teacher—also a Christian—and other men and women at our church with her same skin color, she began to see things differently. She often whispered to me in church, pointing to Yve, Leah, or Sweet, "She so pretty!" Every time these women told Julia she was pretty, I knew the smile on her face was a sign of a heart being healed.

HAVING BUT NOT POSSESSING

"What do you guys want to eat? *Que quieren comer?*" I asked the three girls looking up at me.

"A cheeseburger," said one.

"Chicken nuggets," said another.

"*Una hamburguesa,*" said the third.

"Okay. Go sit down over there. *Siéntate allí,*" I said, pointing to a table right next to the door.

We were a spectacle to behold in our local McDonald's: one white lady spurting out orders in two languages to three smiling girls of different colors. Karen, Emma, and Julia were still full of energy they somehow hadn't burned off at the park. They were excited to be eating at McDonald's, and I was excited to be drinking some caffeine.

At that point, Karen was no longer living with us, but we knew each other so well that it wasn't difficult to revert again into our mother-daughter roles during her weekend sleepover. She was having a blast, and I was grateful for the time together.

On his way out of the restaurant, a dark-skinned man approached us. "Are these girls all yours?" he asked.

Without thinking, I said, "Yes."

"All of them?" he prodded.

"Yup," I said, thinking there was no way I could explain to him the complexities of our relationships in a quick interchange.

Pointing to Julia, he said, "She is really beautiful." He immediately followed that with, "I mean, they are all beautiful."

I smiled. And I thought, *Yes, they are.* Each one was unique with her own beautiful strengths and amazing resilience. They each were teaching me so much, molding my character so distinctly.

I wondered what the girls thought of me telling random strangers that they were "mine." Foster care is a crazy tension that required holding the title of mom with an open hand. Karen didn't really know her mom, so she immediately started calling me mom when she moved into our home. We tried getting her to say "Mama Gena" to recognize there was another mom in her life, even if she hadn't seen her in a long time. It didn't stick. She just called me mom.

Emma had a very close relationship with her mom, so she never once called me mom. I tried hard to make sure that whenever she missed her mom, I reinforced what I knew to be true: "Your mom loves you so much, Emma. I know she misses you a lot."

Julia also had a close relationship with her mom but had already not seen her for four months when she came into our home. The WhatsApp calls helped her understand the depth of her mother's love, and that was important.

In her book *Three Little Words*, Ashley Rhodes-Courter quotes her adoptive mother: "Your mother is a hard act to follow. She will always be the love of your life." I'm convinced that the biological bond between mother and child is one of the strongest forces on earth. As foster moms, we have to assess the best way to fill the role of motherhood without denying this truth. It's one hell of a tension to live in.

One day in late spring, Julia asked, "Can I call you Mom, Gena?"

"Umm, you can call me Mama Gena," I said with an aching heart.

"If I stay here, you'll be my mom," Julia said. "If I go back to Honduras, my mom will be my mom."

"No, your mom will always be your mom, no matter where you are. I'm just taking care of you until we can get you back to her. You're going home to Honduras very soon," I said, hoping it was the right thing to say.

There's this crazy verse in the Bible: "Our hearts ache, but we always have joy. We are poor, but we give spiritual riches to others. We own nothing, and yet we have everything" (2 Corinthians 6:10 NLT). This is what being a foster mom is: letting go of the idea of owning children and yet having them, always with open arms and open hands.

In her book *To the End of June*, Cris Beam says this beautifully as she lists off the wrong reasons people become foster parents.

> You become a foster parent because it's the right thing to do. . . . I think this argument fails because it clashes with our deeply grooved notions of ownership and industry; we don't want children if they can't be ours, and we expect to be rewarded, in the end, for our hard work. Other times I think no child will truly believe she's part of a family if she knows, at heart, she's a charity case.[1]

I recognize that my personal experience as a foster mom is limited. It's easy for me to say that we have to hold our arms open, because I'm not mothering a child whose parents are regularly absent from required weekly family meetings or regularly abuse the child or don't want to be reunited. I know that for foster moms who live in that tension—honoring a child's parents while being honest about where they are is beyond hard. It's incredibly difficult.

A child needs to tangibly see he's someone's even if the audience is just a random stranger at a McDonald's. He needs to know that someone will stand up for him, fight for him, sacrifice for him, protect him, walk him home after he's run away. She needs to know that those arms are open for other mother-like figures in her life, but that they will close tight when danger lurks, regardless of where it comes from.

ASSIMILATION IMBALANCE

Julia decided to pray in my stead one night before bed. "Dear God, thank you for my mom and brothers. And for Grandbe and Gpop, Nonna and Peepa, Crunkle and Tia, Nat and Corey, and for Cade, Juniper, Julia, Andrew, and Gena. Amen."

It didn't take long for Julia to learn English. Going to an English-only school with a beautiful teacher, Katrina—who not only taught her English but also let her teach the class Spanish—benefited Julia greatly. By the time June rolled around, those first days of tears and fighting against entering the school were long gone, replaced by lots of hugs and high-fives with teachers and administrators at her school.

So when Julia decided to pray one night after two months of me praying every night, I wasn't surprised that she prayed in English. In fact, her desire to speak English became a bit worrisome for Andrew and me. "Speak to me in English!" she scolded me one day. "I don't want you to speak Spanish to me."

"But I want to practice my Spanish," I responded.

"I don't want you to speak Spanish to me," she insisted. But I still did.

This was concerning when it paralleled other markers of assimilation. "I don't want to talk to my mom," she would tell me after a few minutes of being on the phone, though her video conversations between her family often lasted hours. This particular time, she continued to talk to her mom, but every ten minutes, she passed me the phone and said, "Tell my mom I don't want to talk to her anymore." Andrew and I encouraged her to keep talking. Of course, if there was a movie on our television, the desire not to talk to her family was even stronger.

In her book *Raise Your Voice*, Kathy Khang, who immigrated to the United States when she was eight months old, discussed the issue of assimilation from her personal experience:

> Assimilation can be seen as selling out your cultural roots while simultaneously be required for survival. . . . I spoke only Korean until I started kindergarten. I used English to excel and fit in at school. I spoke Korean at home and church. For years, I hated my parents for "forcing" me to maintain some ability to speak, read, and write Korean. They were serious—they made their own language learning worksheets for me. Assimilating was necessary due to the teasing and sometimes physical harassment over what I couldn't control, such as my facial features, my last name, and the stereotypes.[2]

With Julia, language was the first domino. All the cultural norms I'd previously wished she'd adapt to suddenly became tainted with this negative label in my mind: assimilation. She began eating sandwiches and not requiring a separate meal of avocados and tortillas. "I don't like avocados anymore," she told me one day.

I was concerned that this would negatively affect her reentry into her home country, which we were working hard to make happen as soon as possible. All the comforts of her current life would change as she dealt with reverse culture shock, a very real emotional and psychological distress that I had experienced often.

Studies show that children are often more affected by reverse culture shock than adults, as they can't fully describe what they're feeling or process it well. An article in the *Journal of Travel Medicine* on a study of culture shock makes the issue clear:

> Intrapersonal factors include age, previous travel experience, language skills, resourcefulness, independence, tolerance and personal appearance. . . . The adolescents in particular presented more behavioral problems on returning home, where people were not interested in their overseas experience and they were not accepted by existing peer groups at school.[3]

Providing a safe and secure home is one thing, but Andrew and I were scared that our home was becoming Julia's cultural space to assimilate. We kept speaking Spanish. We kept eating avocados. We tried to keep her focused on her family while video-chatting.

Three months into our time as her foster family, we were on alert. When I told my social-worker friend Elle, she was grateful I was recognizing it. "Oftentimes, foster parents just want the children to assimilate without recognizing the negative effects of it. Where reunification is the primary goal, foster parents need to be aware of the effects this may have on the children when they return to their own homes," Elle said.

This is an age-old debate. How much should an immigrant assimilate? Laila Lalami sheds light on the issue in her article "What Does It Take to 'Assimilate' in America."

> What does assimilation mean these days? The word has its roots in the Latin "*simulare*," meaning to make similar. Immigrants are expected, over an undefined period, to become like other Americans, a process metaphorically described as a melting pot. But what this means, in practice, remains unsettled. After all, Americans have always been a heterogenous population— racially, religiously, regionally. By what criteria is an outsider

judged to fit into such a diverse nation? . . . It should be clear by now that assimilation is primarily about power. In Morocco, where I was born, I never heard members of Parliament express outrage that French immigrants—or "expats," as they might call themselves—eat pork, drink wine or have extramarital sex, in plain contradiction of local norms. If they do adopt the country's customs or speak its language, they aren't said to have "assimilated" but to have "gone native." In France, by contrast, politicians regularly lament that people descended from North African immigrants choose halal food options for school lunches or want to attend classes in head scarves.[4]

Foster care requires walking a million fine lines. Fostering a refugee on the path to reunification in her home country seemed to add a million more.

Paperwork finally started to come together when the county judge signed off on Julia's reunification. The Honduran consulate finally had all the information it needed to issue travel papers. And Julia's excitement about being back in Honduras exploded upon the news of this paperwork. As we began talking more and more about her return home to Honduras, the grip of assimilation seemed to loosen significantly.

A week before we left to return to Honduras, we talked about one of my favorite commodities. "I can't wait to get home and drink some coffee," Julia said, shaking her head happily.

"I know," I replied.

"Why would you get in trouble if you gave me coffee?"

"It's hard to explain, but it is not something children are allowed to drink here."

"I don't understand why kids can't drink coffee here in this country. It's so good. I like to wake up in the morning and drink it with a piece of bread. I can't wait!"

The day before we left to return to Honduras, I was making sandwiches for lunch when she said to me, "I want a tortilla with avocado and cheese."

Immensely relieved, I merely said, "Okay."

I made a mental note that I needed to talk to Lupe about reverse culture shock and the ways it can manifest. I wanted to make sure we had a conversation about supporting her during the transition. I didn't want her behavior to be translated incorrectly.

LA DESPEDIDA

Several days before we were planning for Julia to return to Honduras, we had a *despedida*—a going-away party. We didn't want to have a theme for the party because we knew that her mom was already planning a welcome-home party for her, and we wanted to be intentional about not overshadowing her party with ours.

We decided to go to a splash park and play in the fountains with friends first, and then go to a park shelter and eat. For about two hours, the kids ran around in the fountains in ninety-three-degree heat. Foster moms and teachers were gathered around the tables with umbrellas, excited to be chatting but maintaining their gaze on the children.

Conversations about biological parents, court proceedings, and social workers were interrupted again and again. "Mom, can I have an ice cream?" "Mom, where's my towel?" "Mom, I'm thirsty!"

When Julia's baby foster cousin arrived, all she wanted to do was pick her up and hold her. She always loved holding babies.

On the way from the splash park to the shelter, Julia got down to business. "Is it my birthday?" she asked.

"No, it's your party because we all love you and will miss you when you go to Honduras."

"Is there a cake?"

"Yes! It's pretty!"

"Can I stick my face in it and somebody push my head down?"

I knew she was referring to a tradition I had often participated in—*la mordida*. She wanted her head pushed into the cake as she was biting it.

"Of course we can do that," I replied.

She sat there gleefully content.

The park shelter was full of the people who had spoken into her life. Our pastor and his wife, our parents, our church community brothers and sisters, nieces and nephews, the foster community, and Julia's school community all came out to celebrate her and the impact she'd had on each of us.

Earlier that day, our church had prayed over our journey, listened to us as we told her story, and discussed the immigration issues in our nation. Our pastor confessed that before our involvement, he'd had a very different perspective on immigration. The depths of the immigration crisis had been discussed at length on social media, but I knew how infrequently it was discussed from the pulpit. Yet it's a topic so interconnected with the gospel. As M. Daniel Carroll R. says in his book *Christians at the Border*,

> In the United States it seems as if it is becoming more and more difficult to be hospitable, to take the time to be with others and welcome them into one's home. Life is so busy and full of activity, and families can be so fractured, that few are able to slow down and open their heart and hearth to anyone, let alone someone different. Nevertheless, to cling to a chosen lifestyle and schedule, define the permitted parameters of a neighborhood, and monopolize time just for oneself and one's family to the exclusion of the stranger—any stranger—might be rebellion against God and an ignoring of something dear to him. The biblical challenge to be hospitable to the stranger is set before the individual Christian and Christian communities, whether large or small.[5]

What our church did that day was open its heart and hearth to our story and to Julia's story. Foster parents often feel alone, even if they do feel called. Having a community open itself up to a foster family is just as necessary as having foster families open up their homes to vulnerable children. When churches become good neighbors and intentional residents of their own counties, the gospel begins to permeate the region, allowing the church to be the living organism of transformation it was always meant to be.

As I looked at the smiling faces that surrounded Julia that hot Sunday afternoon, I stood amazed at how God had connected this little girl to us—and us to the community she needed. Several people there spoke Spanish, several had her same skin color, several were a part of our family. Julia's specific distrust of certain types of human beings had been on display when she first entered our home. I didn't know a lot of details about the life she'd lived in her sponsorship home before us, but I knew enough to see that her distrust was based on experience. I had hoped her time with us would allow her to see her own skin color as beautiful and to have positive interactions with men, especially. She interacted with other human beings who not only treated her with respect but also modeled treating strangers and friends with that same dignity.

That afternoon, as I watched her interact seamlessly with black, brown, and white people, I knew the Lord had intentionally worked against a marred mentality. No, Julia's healing isn't complete, but the divine is on the move within her and around her.

Hot dogs, hamburgers, chips, strawberries, apples, and fruit snacks were served with lemonade. When it came time for cake, we sang her "Happy Birthday" first, even though her birthday was months away. It just seemed right.

In an attempt to compromise between the two cultures so that others would still eat the cake, we cut off a giant piece of her purple-frosted princess cake. Holding back her hair with one hand, I pushed her head into the cake with the other. *La mordida.*

She laughed and laughed.

BEING WITH MOM

Juniper and Julia were having a discussion in the car ride home from school. I explained to Juniper that she wouldn't be traveling with us to Honduras, and Julia added, "I'm sorry, Juniper, but I gotta go see my mom."

"I gotta go see *my* mom," Juniper said. Her response didn't surprise me as her nearly three-year-old self was in a constant state of repeating others.

"Your mom is right here!" Julia exclaimed. "My mom is in Honduras. I gotta go see her! You get to go with Nonna and Peepa and Cade and go swimming."

When I told Julia we had two weeks left, she started dancing, jumping, and shouting. "I get to go see my mom!"

"Yes, sweet girl," I said, having no idea she'd understood it to be two days.

When two days passed, with a frown she said, "You said I get to see my mom today." I explained the difference between days and weeks, and although she was a bit upset, she remained hopeful and perky.

When only two days were left, her excitement skyrocketed. I told her on the way to school, "Today is your last day of school."

"Really? It is?" she said.

"Yes, it is."

"I get to go see my mom? Yay! I get to see my mom! I get to see my mom!" she exclaimed, beaming.

"Today is your last day. Tomorrow we get the travel papers, and the next day we go to the airport. Make sure you squeeze your classmates and your teachers."

The next day came, and we went to the mobile consulate to get the papers. I could hardly believe the day had finally arrived. As we walked through a group of Hondurans waiting in line for consulate services that morning, I couldn't help but wonder what their stories were and if they'd get what they needed to not just survive but thrive.

Nationwide rallies were scheduled to happen that day—June 30, 2018—in protest against the Trump administration's zero-tolerance policy. Earlier that week, on June 26, a federal judge in California had ordered that within thirty days the administration reunite the families they'd separated.[6] I wondered if some of the Hondurans standing in the line at the mobile consulate would later participate in the #FamiliesBelongTogether march in Charlotte, or if they felt it too risky to attend.

The consulate worker led us into a small room with folding chairs and desks. We sat down, and she squeezed her way up to the front, where two workers with computers sat at a white plastic table. She kissed their cheeks and said hello. I tried to eavesdrop on their conversation, but I couldn't hear what they were saying. I also tried to read their body language, wondering how long we'd be there.

The social workers, Andrew, and I weren't convinced that all of our ducks were in a row. We wouldn't have been surprised had the consulate told us we needed to do something more. But before I could think too hard about all the potential problems, the consulate worker called us up to the front. Julia needed to get fingerprinted, and there were smiles all around. This seemed like a good sign.

With tears in my eyes and in the consulate workers' eyes, we received the documentation we needed to travel. "Thank you for what you've done for her," she told us. She then explained all the other documents we needed to take with us while we traveled.

Her coworker took a picture with all of us, and then we were led back out into the parking lot. "Now I get to go see my mom?" Julia asked as we walked back to the car.

"Now we get to take you home," I said emotionally as I sent a message to Lupe to give her the good news.

"Can I have a piece of gum?" Julia asked, totally relaxed and unaware of the miracle we had just witnessed.

I gave a piece of mint-flavored gum as I thought, *Now we need another miracle to find a flight home.*

On the ride home, I searched on my phone to see if the flights we'd been eyeing were still available. We hadn't wanted to purchase the tickets on a mobile phone because we were afraid we'd miss a detail. Andrew and I also discussed all the things we had to do.

We arrived home and hoped a movie would entertain Julia so we could purchase tickets. The flights we'd eyed were gone, which stressed us out. We fought. We searched some more. I stressed out more. We talked to Lupe and tried to figure out a different travel path. We were struggling to find the information we needed on an in-country flight.

I searched and searched. Andrew told me to let it go and just plan on flying in two days, when we could get the flight we needed. I told him to let me search for another fifteen minutes. But I searched for two more hours. I didn't want to tell Lupe we couldn't travel the next day. She'd been waiting for months to see her precious daughter. Andrew and I fought some more, and finally I gave up. I sent a message to Lupe with the bad news.

"It's okay, Gena," she wrote. "It's in God's timing. Who knows why things happen as they do, but the important thing is she has the papers to fly home, and I'll see you in two days."

I had just witnessed another miracle: a mother's patience that defied all logic.

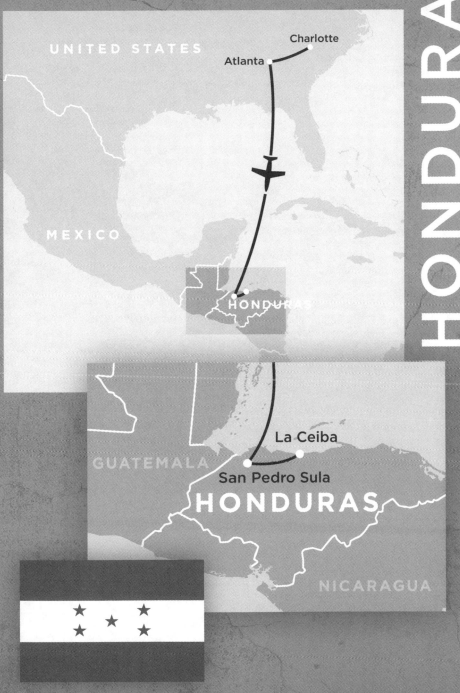

PART 4

HONDURAS

UNITED STATES

Charlotte

Atlanta

MEXICO

HONDURAS

GUATEMALA

La Ceiba

San Pedro Sula

HONDURAS

NICARAGUA

Chapter Nine

REUNIFICATION/ *REUNIFICACIÓN*

JULIA, LUPE, GENA, AND ANDREW: JULY 2018

POR LLEGAR (EN ROUTE)

The alarm went off at three in the morning. We had put Julia to bed early the night before, but we had all been a bit restless. She woke up twice during the night and ended up sleeping in our bed with us for about an hour.

In the past, she'd often had nightmares involving snakes. She'd wake up in the morning and tell me, "I dreamt about snakes again." One time, she gave details. "Andrew and you were there, and Andrew killed the snake!" she told me smiling. I reassured her that we would protect her.

That night, not long after Julia went to bed, Andrew had found a black snake on our front porch. He didn't kill it, but he did move it away from our house.

The next morning, he asked Julia how she slept. He'd often ask our kids that, prompting them to be creative. "Did you sleep like a rock? Like a giraffe? Like a turtle?" he'd ask. That morning, Julia had a new response. "I slept like a star, a princess star," she said proudly. "And I didn't dream of any snakes!"

As we pulled out of our driveway at four, we knew it'd be a while before she fell back asleep. "I'm going to see my mom!" she said excitedly. "I'm not going to live at your house anymore, but it's okay. You, Andrew, Cade, and Juni will still be with me, because we can talk on video."

My stomach was a mess with a deep nervousness I'd never felt before. It felt like pressure in my womb. I wondered how often we'd get stopped along the route and if our pile of unique papers would protect us against the snakes that surrounded bureaucratic pigeon-holes. Andrew was nervous too.

Before boarding the first plane from Charlotte to Atlanta, Julia began to reflect a bit more. "So I'm not going to have a trampoline anymore, because my house doesn't have a trampoline."

I asked, "No, but having your mom is better than having a trampoline, right?"

"Yes!" she said, showing off her top row of teeth. I hoped our house full of tangible comforts and American entertainment would have no hold over her.

As the plane took off, Julia's eyes were glued to the window next to her. She giggled. "I'm so happy to go see my mommy!"

Ms. Adrienne, her school administrator, had given her a sticker activity book at her going-away party, saying, "You can't use this until the plane ride." Julia had tried several times to persuade me to let her play with it, but to no avail. I pulled it out, and she happily drew in it.

Periodically she looked out the window. "*Nieve*," she said excitedly at the clouds.

"No, honey, that's not snow. Those are *nubes*—clouds," I said.

She gave me a confused look for good reason, as the clouds look impressively like a blanket of snow. A few seconds later she pointed at them again. "*Nube*," she said with confidence.

At the gate in Atlanta for our flight to San Pedro Sula, Honduras, Julia overheard the flight attendant announcing the details and yelled, "I heard her say Honduras!" When we started boarding, Julia began a joyful singsong chant:

I want my mommy!
I want my mommy!

I love my mommy!
I love my mommy!
I'm going to my mommy!
Lupe. Lupe. Lupe.

Right before the plane took off for San Pedro Sula, Julia stopped playing Angry Birds and leaned toward me. "I want to take a nap," she said. She rarely volunteered to take a nap or go to bed at all, so we took advantage of her admission.

I loosened her seatbelt a bit and raised the armrest between us, and she laid her head on my left thigh. She squirmed and positioned her feet to the right spot. I began to caress her curly onyx hair. Within minutes she was asleep. As she rested on me, I laid my head on Andrew's shoulder and snaked my right arm around his left arm. Never in my wildest dreams could I have imagined this man that I'd known since ninth grade would be there with me then, a part of this wild story. I couldn't think of anyone else more equipped. I couldn't imagine anywhere safer than next to him.

Julia awoke not long before the plane was flying above Cancún, Mexico. The three of us gawked at the turquoise expanse below us. "Look at that water!" Julia exclaimed.

Andrew and I were five months away from celebrating ten years of marriage. Our plan was to put our toes in that turquoise water, as we'd never gotten to visit Cancún while living near Monterrey, Mexico. "You must go!" we had been advised on several occasions by our Mexican friends.

Andrew locked eyes with mine as we flew over that item on our bucket list. I knew our doubts were the same. "At least now I've seen it," he said.

A decade before, our vows were merely hopeful words about an unseen future: "I will encourage you to appreciate deeper depths, higher heights, and wider widths of Christ's love. I give you my honesty and my kindness, and I vow to seek the kingdom of God first above all else." On that plane ride, it was clear those words had become the body and blood of a covenant between us, a living testament—full of tension and humanity and struggle—that Christ's love is as inclusive as it is radical, as authentic as it is extravagant, as human as it is divine.

When we went through customs in Honduras, we felt we were at the mercy of the customs agent. After hearing our story and looking at Julia's travel papers, she got up to go talk to a manager. We waited, wondering what would happen next. When she returned, she said we could go, but she'd need to keep the original travel document with her.

I was so thankful Andrew had asked me to make a copy of it before our travels.

A little nervous, we made our way to the local airline desk to get our boarding passes for our third flight. The attendants were not happy about us bringing a copy of Julia's birth certificate. Policy required an original. We told our story again. A man took our passports and a few other papers and told us he had to go get a security clearance. When he walked out of sight with that important documentation, our nervousness increased.

A few minutes later, he came back and gave us clearance, handing all of our documents back to us.

We were one flight away from Lupe.

When we arrived, we called her. "I'm five minutes away," she said. We got our luggage and waited. Five minutes turned into thirty. We scrutinized every car that came into the airport. A red Jeep. A taxi. A black SUV. *No, that woman is moving too slowly to be her. She'd be running,* I thought. A white sedan. A yellow sedan. Another taxi. A black pickup.

Another white sedan parked in the front row. Lupe got out of the front passenger seat and began running toward the door. Julia saw her as soon as I did. Andrew and I had our phones out ready to record, and Julia started jumping and yelping, crying and laughing.

"Mommy!" she yelled and ran out to meet her. Julia stopped at the top of the steps and waited for Lupe to climb them. With eyes squinted and tears falling fast, Lupe wrapped her arms around her daughter. "*Te amo mija*," she said. "I love you, my daughter." Then she picked up Julia like she was a baby and wrapped Julia's legs around her body.

She gave Andrew and me hugs as well as she could with Julia still attached to her. As we got in the car, she sat Julia on her lap, where she remained for the three-hour drive home. Julia chewed her watermelon-flavored gum and offered her mom some. We laughed, smiled till our mouths hurt, and shared stories.

"Last night I went to a funeral," Lupe told me. "An eighteen-year-old boy died in our community from a motorcycle accident. I had to go pay my respects to his mom. Here I am happy because my daughter has returned. But she's crying for her child who is gone forever."

LA BIENVENIDA (THE WELCOME)

"*Libre soy, libre soy. Libertad sin vuelta atrás!*" boomed from Lupe's back patio. As parents of little girls, we immediately recognized it as the Spanish version of "Let It Go," the theme song from the Disney movie *Frozen*. Five little Elsa lookalikes flocked to Julia as she got out of the car. I barely had a chance to hug and say hi to her brothers before I was excavating Julia's luggage to find her Elsa dress and white high-heeled shoes, which we had for this moment. Within minutes, she was dressed, and Lupe was fixing her hair.

"The crown?" Lupe yelled out at me from a sea of Elsas. I turned around and began excavating some more. I emerged to a see little five-year-old girl who had been transformed into someone I wasn't sure I recognized: hair down and spritzed, bright-red lipstick, and a flowing train on her ice queen dress. Lipstick was not an option in our home, and I wondered if her mom let it slide as part of the party.

I went back outside and took in the sights: rented plastic tables and chairs, neighborhood friends and family sitting and talking, Elsa centerpieces that I was sure Lupe handmade, Julia's brothers moving to and fro, making sure everything was in its place. Against the concrete wall between Lupe's yard and her neighbor's sat the main table with an Elsa cake and cupcakes. Behind the table was a white background lined with three rows of white and blue balloons above blue and silver streamers tied off like window curtains to reveal blue Styrofoam letters spelling out Julia's name and the word "Welcome" in English.

Enrique, Julia's seventeen-year-old brother, was all smiles and had his hair in braids. We hugged. "I like your hair," I told him.

He replied, "When we video-chatted, Julia said she wanted my hair to be in braids when she came home, so today I went and had it done."

It became clear to me that this wasn't just a special display of Enrique's love for Julia. It's how he was: sweet and loving. He seemed very mature for his age, but it didn't surprise me. He had always been attentive toward Julia when they chatted on video. As I learned more of his own story, including the role he had to play as the man of the house and caretaker of his great-grandparents, I was amazed at his resilience, his passion for his family, and his love and admiration for his mother and his sister. When we talked a bit about his mom, he said, "She's been through a lot. She's very strong."

I sat down at one of the tables and met twelve-year-old Mateo. He asked me where we lived in the United States and told me his own family's story. Eleven years before, his mom and dad had migrated to Florida, leaving him and his now sixteen-year-old brother to live with their aunt. The parents were trying to get the paperwork for Mateo and his brother to emigrate. He had two siblings he'd never seen face to face, as they were born in Florida.

On the drive from the airport, Andrew sat in the front passenger seat and talked with the driver. His girlfriend had gone north with their daughter, who was three years old at the time. He hadn't seen them for three years. Later we learned of a boy from the community who had recently died in the desert, trying to cross over.

The joy of the occasion was offset by the heaviness of what was typical conversation in that land. Family separation wasn't new; a horrible zero-tolerance policy had made it more common. I wanted to tear my clothes and wail when I heard the stories. But there'd be no national protests against family separation. Choosing to live life every day with family far away was its own version of protest against the cruel realities of family separation. Enrique said that when Lupe found out Julia was found by the police, "she thought she had lost Julia forever."

About two months prior to our arrival, a Honduran dad died by suicide in Texas while he was in the custody of Customs and Border Protection. He had crossed over with his wife and three-year-old son and asked to apply for asylum. The *Washington Post* reported, "Border Patrol agents told the family they would be separated. That's when Muñoz 'lost it,' according to one agent . . . 'They had to use physical force to take the child out of his hands.'"[1]

Lupe also confessed her desire to die when she was separated from her daughter. "But if I don't take care of my children, who will?"

Tamales were served. Then nachos con frijoles (refried beans), sausages, and cupcakes while the *pollo asado* (grilled chicken) was sitting on the grill being fanned by Enrique, Fernando, a neighbor, and at times, Andrew. The entire *Frozen* soundtrack was on repeat. I was impressed at how similar the Spanish voice of each character was to their English counterparts.

Julia danced with the other Elsas, rode piggyback on Enrique, popped balloons with Samuel, and posed for photos in front of her welcome sign. The electricity was flickering on and off, so the landlady and a teenage electrician worked on it inside the house. There was so much commotion it was hard to keep up, as exhausted as we already were. At one point I spoke to Mateo's brother in English without realizing it. He stared at me blankly. I realized what I had done and asked his forgiveness.

It probably came as no surprise to anyone there that Andrew and I made our way to our room immediately after most of the guests left. It was 1 a.m. our time, and we were thoroughly exhausted. Not surprisingly, Julia stayed up after we went to bed, and she was awake the next morning before us.

EL RÍO (THE RIVER)

"Drinking coffee with a little piece of bread is very good," said Julia's ninety-three-year-old great-grandmother the next morning as we sat together chatting. I smiled at the similarities between the two, having heard similar words come from Julia's mouth just a few weeks before.

In that backyard, a cement roof covered an open space where chairs and an old bed sat on gravel. During our time there, the bed was used as a place to play Spot It, a card game where one lays down two cards and has to determine what one object is on both cards. After washing my face in the outdoor laundry sink, I found Andrew playing with the boys while Lupe was cooking breakfast.

They decided the game should move up to the roof, so they got a tall, wobbly ladder and leaned it up against the roof. We all climbed up. The avocado tree suddenly seemed like a bush, and Andrew pointed out an avocado that was as big as an eggplant. As the boys played Spot It on the floor of the roof, I looked out at the mountains on the horizon. Greens of every shade were displayed on stalks, palms, and branches between me and the mountains, with corrugated tin roofs dispersed in between.

The maroon-tiled ground of the back porch that had served as a dance floor the night before was transformed into the dining room that morning. We sat on the floor and ate freshly made tortillas, avocados just picked from the tree, and an egg-and-ham mixture that affirmed Julia's bragging about her mother's cooking.

Seeing Julia interact with her brothers—especially the youngest, Samuel, who played with her new toys as if they were his own—had me reflecting on a phrase she often asked at our house. "Whose is that?" she would ask about drinks, food, and toys. If I responded with "mine," she would then ask a follow-up question. "Is that only for you?" Most times, the answer was an affirmative.

I realized that in her home, what was hers also belonged to her brothers, be it a toy, towel, bed, or room. As the only girl, her clothes were hers alone, but if she'd had sisters, they would have been shared property. So most possessions in her home environment were shared while most possessions at our house were owned by one person, including many of the toys. Thankfully she didn't seem to mind Samuel's dual possession of her things. I hoped she was embracing her new reality.

As Lupe began to wash the dishes from the morning meal in the outside sink, Andrew stepped up to help her and said, "You've been working all morning. I'll do dishes."

"No, Andrew," Lupe said. "When I come to your house, you'll look after me well. And I won't do any dishes there, right?"

"Absolutely," he said. "I hope you can come. You are welcome any time."

Lupe asked us if we'd like to go swimming in the river nearby. It was her birthday, and it seemed like a special treat for all of us. "Is this the river that Julia used to swim in a lot?" I asked, remembering the first time I gave her a bath and saw that she was no stranger to water.

"Yes!" Lupe said excitedly. "It's a long walk there, and it's hot today, but we'll bring our lunch and cook it there."

First Julia and Samuel took a bath. Then they ran around naked. I thought about how challenging it had been for us to get Julia to close the door in our house when she went to the bathroom. We knew the rules of our house were very different from Lupe's rules, but it was enlightening to see how vast those differences were.

Unsure of how deep the river was, and aware that there'd likely be no other women in swimsuits, I decided to go in my jeans and tank top. Andrew changed into his swimming trunks.

I grabbed the bug spray I'd bought and walked onto the back patio. Shirtless, Julia followed and asked if she could spray me. I complied and then sprayed her. Julia then put on one of her bathing suits. Lupe prepared the food and had the older boys run to the store for sodas. As we made our way toward the river, more people joined us. By the time we arrived at our picnicking spot, there were a dozen of us.

Andrew decided to bring our important things with us: passports, telephones, and money. I disagreed but relented. The truth was, we had no idea which would be safer: to bring them with us or to leave them at her house.

After a twenty-minute walk through town, we passed through an area of fly-infested trash and then arrived at a riverbed of boulders and broken rock fragments. A wide greenish-brown river that seemed to originate at the feet of some far-off green-and-blue mountain was already refreshing Hondurans of all ages from the ninety-one-degree heat.

Andrew approached me with a warning and a smile: "We have to cross to get to where we are going to eat."

"Oh, okay," I responded, realizing that the river would come up to my shoulders. Life is an adventure. Flexibility in the unknown makes it more enjoyable.

Andrew and I had packed as many of Julia's things as we could in the two large suitcases we brought. We had our backpacking packs for our own things, so space was limited. On the way to Honduras, I'd dressed up fancier than I ever had before to look the role of educated foster parent rather than hippie traveler, which is what I normally looked like in airports. Instead of bringing my Chaco sandals, which had always been my preferred travel shoes, I chose a pair of dress sandals plus a pair of flip-flops because of how flat they could pack. The river adventure made me especially miss my Chacos—a durable pair of outdoor sandals with synthetic straps that dry quickly. So I crossed the sixty-foot-wide river in my flip-flops, slipping only a few times and catching myself. My body was soaked from my shoulders down. It felt good. Real good.

Then we climbed up a hilly tributary that fed into river. I was glad Andrew had long before introduced me to rock climbing; otherwise I would have been scared. By the time I arrived at the top, one of the family's friends was on the other side of the water, moving rocks and sticks to create a cooking spot. Above him were thick brown roots of healthy, green trees that jutted out from the rock wall.

He had brought a bag of coal up with him and was already fanning it in preparation. To his right and left were deep natural reservoirs. The one on his left was at the same level as us, while the one on the right was several feet below us. I sat across the tributary from the cook in a crevice of rock that seemed like a natural seat. If the Sabbath were a place, that would be it.

Samuel ran past me and jumped off the cliff into the lower reservoir. Fernando did a cartwheel-like jump into it. I smiled as I thought about how much Cade would have loved to join in—and how scared I would've been if he had.

Before long, Lupe was cooking again. She handed over plates full of beans, plantains, sausages, and avocados. Fernando served us cola in blue plastic cups. After we ate, Julia, Samuel, Andrew, Enrique, Fernando, and the others ran up to us and down to the river in random intervals.

After a while, Lupe reclined on her towel, and we talked about trauma and about Julia's time with her sponsorship family. (The sponsorship mother was a good friend of Lupe's.) She speculated about why Marta, her former friend, had mistreated Julia. We talked about cultural differences and about how she hoped Julia could forget the bad things that happened to her in the United States, specifically the neglect in Marta's home.

Julia came running back up and sat with us for a while. After talking a bit about crossing the border, Lupe asked Julia, "What happened after you crossed the river with Carlos?"

Julia was silent for a while. "I don't remember, Mom." That was so unlike her. She had an answer for everyone and everything. She had an answer even before anyone had a question.

"After the nice man gave you pizza and you had to leave me, what happened?" Lupe asked.

"Mom, I don't remember."

Lupe seemed frustrated. Once again, I couldn't imagine being in her shoes. I didn't know a lot of Spanish vocabulary for trauma, but I tried my best. "It may be a protection mechanism of her brain," I said. "A way to protect herself against the trauma."

Unfortunately this was the first I'd heard of Julia's memory loss. I'd never tried to pry information out of her; I'd let her lead conversations about her past. We never once talked about the border. Her therapist in the United States seemed to think she was fine. Andrew and I didn't agree and asked to get a new therapist after several weeks. With the consulate suggesting we'd be taking Julia home in early June, we never got a new therapist for lack of time.

RECOVERING FROM TRAUMA

The International Society for Traumatic Stress Studies provides the following information about childhood trauma and recovering memories:

People forget names, dates, faces and even entire events all the time. But is it possible to forget terrible experiences such as being raped? Or beaten? The answer is yes—under certain circumstances. For more than a hundred years, doctors, scientists and other observers have reported the connection between trauma and forgetting. But only in the past ten years have scientific studies demonstrated a connection between childhood trauma and amnesia.

Most scientists agree that memories from infancy and early childhood—under the age of two or three—are unlikely to be remembered. Research shows that many adults who remember being sexually abused as children experienced a period when they did not remember the abuse. Scientists also have studied child victims at the time of a documented

Julia went back down to the river, and Lupe and I continued talking. For the first time since we'd arrived, Lupe was sitting still and resting. I told her she may see other things in Julia, like not wanting to talk to us on video, being disobedient, or acting out. I tried to explain culture shock and reverse culture shock. I expressed my concern that Julia wasn't just moving houses and house rules—microcultures—but also countries and country rules as well—macrocultures. Later, when Andrew and I video-chatted with Cade and Juniper, Julia didn't want to say hi—and Lupe didn't like it. I reminded her it was likely some type of culture shock, so she didn't need to worry. (By the time we got back to the United States, Julia had sent audio messages to both our kids, along with dozens of heart emojis.)

At one river, Julia had to learn how to protect herself. At that river, her mother had been taken from her. The Rio Grande was where Julia

traumatic event, such as sexual abuse, and then measured how often the victims forget these events as they become adults. They discovered that some people do forget the traumatic experiences they had in childhood, even though it was established fact that the traumatic events occurred.

At the time of a traumatic event, the mind makes many associations with the feelings, sights, sounds, smells, taste and touch connected with the trauma. Later, similar sensations may trigger a memory of the event. While some people first remember past traumatic events during therapy, most people begin having traumatic memories outside therapy.

A variety of experiences can trigger the recall. Reading stories about other people's trauma, watching television programs that depict traumatic events similar to the viewer's past experience, experiencing a disturbing event in the present, or sitting down with family and reminiscing about a terrible shared episode—for some people, these kinds of experiences can open the floodgates of frightful and horrible memories.[2]

had to learn to be an adult in ways no five-year-old should. But this river—her river—had revived her childlike self. She giggled and ran, played and splashed, piggybacked her brothers, and ate several cups of green gelatin. This river—the one where she had learned to swim, to bathe, to clean clothes, to jump off rocks, and to hold her breath—baptized her again on that day. She was a new creation of her former self, and while her trauma did not disappear, it also did not hold her back from being a wide-open child.

NUESTRA ÚLTIMA CENA (OUR LAST SUPPER)

Spot It was a huge hit, and though we were at Julia's house for only three nights and two full days, we played more Spot It than we ever had before.

Fernando came into the living room the next morning full of smiles and said proudly, "I'm starting to learn words in English."

"Really?" I asked.

"Spider—*araña*. Tree—*árbol*."

"Now you can play Spot It in English!"

"Yes!" he said.

Julia looked around the room and started naming off things she saw in English. "Book. Couch. Elsa. TV. Balloon." She had recently expressed her frustration with everyone's amazement that she could speak English. "'Oooh,' they say to me," she said, annoyed.

I replied, "Well it's very strange for them, because when you left, you didn't know any English and now you know a lot!"

Lupe asked me if I wanted to go with her, Julia, and their neighbor Sarai into town to get a few *recuerdos* (souvenirs) before we left the next morning. I happily joined them. Andrew and the boys played soccer at the field a block from their house. The heavy rain that came and went and came again didn't stop them.

We went to the mall and found the souvenir table. Lupe was asking me the names of all the people that had shown love to Julia, and the merchant asked me to write them down, as no one could understand what I was saying: Nonna, Peepa, Grandbe, and Gpop. While names were being engraved on leather keychains, two elementary-school boys came up to us asking for pesos.

I told them I didn't have any, as I had carried no money with me. Lupe's countenance fell when she looked at the boys. Then she asked one of the boys a question I was surprised by: "Where is your mom?" Lack of family is a deep poverty, and Lupe knew that all too well.

I was too far away to hear the boy's response, but I saw Lupe take out some pesos and give them to him. In our posse, she was the only one who gave them money.

We all sat down at a Dunkin' Donuts, where Sarai treated us all to a coffee.

"Do I have to sit right in this chair?" Julia asked me in English. Squirming and jumping around was against the rules in my house, my culture, my country, so she needed to know if that rule applied there. So I responded, "Not unless your mom says so." Julia continued to squirm, and her mother said nothing. I smiled, grateful Julia was understanding that she was no longer under my maternal authority.

Sarai talked about volunteering at a local orphanage, where she went often to teach the girls baking skills. I asked, "What motivated you to volunteer there?"

"My dad left and went to the United States when I was eight years old," she said. "I still had a father, but he wasn't present at an age that a child needs her father." Her father returned home when she was a teenager after being deported. "I'm always aware of children who don't have parents or whose parents aren't in their lives."

We then went to the grocery store to get meat for Sarai's mom to make us Honduran tacos, which looked a lot to me like Mexican flautas. On the way to the store, Lupe saw a friend on the other side of the street. "Look, Hector! *Mi hija ya regresó!* (My daughter is back!)" she shouted out to him.

We arrived at Sarai's house to a room full of people: Andrew and the boys were there, plus Abram (Sarai's brother who was with us at the river) and Sarai's father, mother, other brother, sister-in-law, and nephew.

Andrew and Abram had several conversations about agriculture. Abram's family had plants all around their backyard, and he showed off each one, sharing its name and characteristics. Andrew, a green thumb himself, spent a lot of time with Abram, discussing the politics and economics of Honduran agriculture.

The women began making tacos while the men sat around the TV and talked. Julia's great-grandmother came over, and we arranged the chairs on the front patio so we could all sit in a circle, eat tacos, and drink fresh lemonade. This was the Honduras I remembered well and missed often: community celebrated around a meal. We heard stories of how these neighbors had helped Lupe a lot over the past year: giving her boys snacks from their little store, even when she didn't have the money; sharing their Wi-Fi with her so she could speak to Julia; letting Samuel run errands with them so Lupe could accomplish her daily tasks.

When everyone had gone to bed, I asked Lupe about her interaction with the boys at the mall. "What moved you about those boys?"

"They reminded me of my own situation," she responded. I wasn't sure if she was talking about Julia being away from her, about her own broken childhood, or both.

"You care about children a lot. That is very clear," I said. "From the neighborhood kids who came to eat with us at the river to the boys at the mall. You are a great mom. You are amazing."

She was planning to tell me more about her time in Mexico that night, but it seemed the Spirit was moving in a different direction. I held her hands in mine and prayed for her: for strength, for peace, for protection, and for friends to confide in. When I laid my head down after our prayer, I felt a deep sense of gratefulness that Lupe and I were friends.

The next morning, Andrew sat outside with Enrique for a bit. Enrique had taken care of his great-grandfather while Lupe was being held hostage at the border. When Raquel, Lupe's aunt, quit giving him medicine, Enrique visited him in the hospital every day, right up until he died in late winter of 2018, prior to Lupe's return. Sarai's family had helped Enrique with the funeral and with taking care of Fernando and Samuel. It was the first time he'd had a close relative die, and he'd carried that emotional burden without his mom around.

He told Andrew, "You and Gena showed me the love of God more than anyone in my life. You took care of Julia like she was your own."

Lupe and I had a similar conversation not long after. "This is what I could not understand," she said. "How could a family of strangers take care of my daughter as if they were family? You loved her like she was one of your own children."

Jesus came to earth to make a way for all of us to be part of his family. The gospel is the good news that strangers can become family, despite their many differences.

SAYING GOODBYE

Goodbyes came after breakfast. Lupe, Enrique, Fernando, Samuel, Julia, Andrew, and I all cried. Abram and his mother came over to take a picture of us. Afterward we went inside the house and finished packing our things. Lupe asked if she could pray with us before we left, so the seven of us linked hands and stood in the living room, sniffling. Andrew began the prayer. (Unlike me, he was always good at praying in Spanish.) Lupe finished with her own prayer. Abram came in halfway through the prayer and stretched his arms over the boys. After the prayer, he took Lupe into the kitchen to ask her something privately.

When they returned, he said that he and his father would drive Andrew and me to our hotel that night, two hours away. "It's safer," he said. The whole family had been concerned the night before when we told them which hotel we would be staying at. "Ask the bus driver to let you off here," they told me. "Getting a taxi from where the bus normally stops will be very expensive."

We were very grateful. In the emotional heaviness of the whole trip, it was hard to focus on details, and having trusted friends to drive us relieved much stress. We said our goodbyes to everyone but Samuel, who had found a way to join us on our ride.

When we tried to give Abram and his father money for gas, they wouldn't take it. When we realized along the way that we had the wrong name for the hotel, they simply laughed and drove us where we needed to go.

Finally, at our hotel, after all our goodbyes were given, I sank in the comfortable bed, remembering Julia's words from earlier that morning:

"Is this your last day?" she asked.

"Yes. After breakfast we have to leave," I said.

She hugged me. "But I want to be with you," she'd said, her voice full of longing.

"I know, honey. I want to be with you too. But now you are home." I was crying.

With no tears, she took my face in her hands and said, "I know you have gum."

Laughing through the tears, like the sun bursting through the clouds, I replied, "Do you want a piece?"

"Yes!" she exclaimed.

Chapter Ten

REFLECTIONS

LANGUAGE

The language we use. "*Alien* has been used since the eighteenth century both in legislation and by the courts," said Robert Stribley in a *Huffington Post* article.

Tracing its origins in United States law also reveals some disturbing twists. Its first federal use came when we developed legislation to determine who could become a citizen. Who were these lucky, select aliens? Only those who could be described as a "free white person." That was codified in our 1790 Alien Naturalization Act enacted by Congress in 1790.[1]

On a tour of the Port Isabela Detention Center in McAllen, Texas, an ICE officer showed my group one dormitory that held seventy-five beds, two vending machines, pay phones along the wall, and a bathroom. "The aliens also get one dollar a day for the work they do if they choose to do a work detail," the officer said. His coldness toward immigrants was evident from the moment he introduced himself. Two of his colleagues confessed they had to turn off their emotions to do their job.

I couldn't help but think that calling immigrants "aliens" was a psychological tool not just to demean immigrants but also to decrease turnover of federal personnel, dehumanizing them and stripping away their emotional capacity to see others as human. As my fellow tour-taker Tess Clarke, cofounder of Seek the Peace and strategist for We Welcome Refugees, said, "That term is the most foreign one we can apply to the 'other,' and it allows us to continue to believe we don't exist in the same universe, thus justifying inhumane treatment and dehumanization."

Francisco Cantú, who wrote *The Line Becomes a River*, said this about his experience as a Border Patrol agent:

> The turnover rate is very high. The suicide rate is proportionate with other law enforcement careers. But in the border patrol there isn't a culture of talking about the way you might be impacted by the trauma or the violence of the job. I've shared this book with a handful of my former colleagues and most of them will say to me: "Oh, wow, I didn't know you were going through so much," or: "I didn't know you were having a hard time." And it's true, I never talked about it. I never talk about the nightmares I had with any of those guys. No matter where you stand on border policy, the job that border patrol agents are asked to do is extremely difficult and also kind of insane. I don't think you have to become soulless in order to do the work, but I do think it is work that endangers the soul.[2]

Likewise, the word *illegal* is often used and is argued to be a valid way to describe an immigrant with unauthorized status in the United States. In all other cases, *illegal* is used as an adjective to describe an action, not a human. Beyond being immoral, that term leads to more confusion about the topic, as many people assume that one's legal status is black and white. But the reality is much more nuanced, as immigration is fluid. Immigration rights activist Jose Antonio Vargas wrote in an article for *Time*, "In a country that believes in due process of the law, calling an immigrant illegal is akin to calling a defendant awaiting trial a criminal."[3] Vargas asks why we don't call drunk drivers illegals or underage drivers illegals. "In what other contexts do we call someone illegal?"[4]

I will address some action steps in the "What Can We Do" section. But we'll start with the first action step here: intentionally becoming aware of the language we use and actively refraining from using dehumanizing language. If we truly believe the *imago Dei* is imprinted on every human being, we can't continue to call other human beings by subhuman titles. As Jesus said, what comes out of our mouths is what defiles us (Matthew 15:11).

Mother language and interconnectedness. My white culture didn't teach me that women are directly connected to the earth. Yet hidden in our language are the treasures of such a connection: Mother Earth, Mother Nature, motherland. This connection is made clear in a book our Honduran friend Abram gave us, *Voces, Silencios y Cicatrices de la Violencia Contra Las Mujeres (Voices, Silences, and Scars of the Violence Against Women)*. It shows how the violence suffered by women does both social and environmental harm. The book, which aims to "defend those who defend mother earth and the natural resources in Honduras," shares the sobering stories of abuse suffered by twenty women whose lives and organizations work hard to protect the environment. In 1999, Honduras began allowing twenty-two American, Canadian, and European companies to explore and exploit the land. Since 2002, mining has tripled in the country.[5]

We saw this in person when Abram showed us his community's mountain being mined. When we went to the river, Lupe explained that the brown water was much clearer before the mining began.

Voces, Silencios y Cicatrices also discusses the correlation between human rights and the environment, bringing to light the struggle for life in connection to "the earth, the rivers and hydraulic resources, the ancestral lands and human rights in general."[6]

Additionally, [the book] seeks to contribute to the visibility of these violent acts that women suffer that make it even harder to insert themselves in the social fight, to give conscience to the need for promoting changes in the power relationship between the genders, between men and women in everyday routines, in the organizational structures, in communities, and in public.[7]

Though the book doesn't use the term *ecofeminism*, it opened my understanding of it. However similar to the term *feminism*, it isn't as inclusive as it should be, especially toward women of color.

Ecofeminism refers to the deep connection between females and Mother Earth, revealed in the life-giving power of women, fertile or not. I'm grateful for the Latina women in my life who have spoken this truth to me. In her book *Mujerista Theology*, Ada María Isasi-Díaz writes about the liturgy that was spoken at LAS HERMANAS Conference in San Antonio, Texas, in 1989. The song "Lucha, Poder, Esperanza," composed for the conference, speaks to this deep connection.

Lucha, Poder, Esperanza	Struggle, power, hope,
Mujer Hispana en tu vientre	Hispanic woman in your womb,
llevas semillas del Verbo.	you carry seeds of the Word.
¡Demos vida al continente!	Let's give life to the continent.
Adelante compañeras	Onward, *compañeras,*
que a nuestro pueblo asesinan	they are murdering our people
y a la tierra nuestra madre	and our mother, the earth.
el imperio ultraja y viola.	The empire is ravaging and raping.
Vamos a unirnos, hermanas	Let us come together, sisters,
firmes, valientes, ya basta	firmly, bravely. It is enough!
de ser esclavas del miedo	No longer slaves of fear we'll be
hijas de raza violada.	nor daughters of a raped race.
Al viento nadie lo para	No one stops the wind,
al mar nadie lo encadena	no one chains the sea.
las mujeres solidarias	The women in solidarity
son fuego que nadie apaga.	are a fire no one can extinguish.

Tu causa es causa del Pueblo,	Your cause is the people's cause,
tu dignidad es sagrada	your dignity is sacred.
mujer color de la tierra	Woman, your color is the earth's.
árbol de la vida nueva.	You are tree of new life.
Lucha, poder, esperanza	Struggle, power, hope
sea consigna en la batalla	may it be the cry of our struggle
por rescatar la justicia	to rescue justice,
nuestra hermana aprisionada.	our imprisoned sister.[8]

Isasi-Díaz explains that *mujerista* theology believes "the coming of the kin-dom of God has to do with a coming together of peoples, with no one being excluded and at the expense of no one."[9] In regard to immigration, we must all work together toward justice (excluding no one and including unaccompanied minors). As Valeria Luiselli says,

> The whole thing is a mess, a puzzle impossible to piece together using common sense and logic. But this much is clear: until all the governments involved—the American, Mexican, Salvadoran, Honduran, and Guatemalan governments, at least—acknowledge their shared accountability in the roots and causes of the children's exodus, solutions to the crisis will be impossible.[10]

Ultimately we are each connected to the ground we come from and the ground we live on—whether we're immigrants or not—and we must collectively rescue our sister Justice, whose chains affect women, men, children, and the ground that connects us all. The country we each live in—whether the United States, Mexico, Honduras, or another—is "as beautiful as it is broken, and we are somehow now part of it, so we are also broken with it, and feel ashamed, confused, and sometimes hopeless, and are trying to figure out how to do something about all that."[11]

While borders may hold our distinct heritage, culture, and language, they don't keep us from connecting with those from other heritages, other cultures, and other languages. The Earth is the Lord's, not ours. And the fullness within this planet God has given us is meant for building community and creating shalom between *us* and *them*, between humans and Mother Earth, between women and men, between unaccompanied minors and Border Patrol, between black lives and blue uniforms, between foster moms and biological moms, between those who are oppressors and those who are oppressed—and everyone in between who has dual roles.

This is the work of the Lord. Shalom in its fullness is right relationship between humans and themselves, humans and other humans, humans and God, and humans and the environment. This is the renewal of life; this is the new Earth that will one day mother us all.

The call to Christians is to work for and usher in shalom here and now while simultaneously *esperando* (waiting for or hoping for) the renewal of all things when the upside-down kin-dom comes for good.

WHAT CAN WE DO?

Look and lament. Michelle Warren, who led the women I went with to the border, urged us to *perceive*. She challenged us not to plan what we could do but to look and perceive first. I was grateful for the countercultural call she gave us. In his interview with *The Guardian*, Francisco Cantú said, "I have no urge to look away from the border, not just our border but borders globally. I think they're sort of these microcosms of all of these painful, beautiful, violent, incomprehensible mysteries of our modern lives. We're embodied by them."[12] It's too easy to look away. We must take time to perceive what's going on at the border.

On the flight home from McAllen, Texas, after walking through Ursula Processing Center and Port Isabel Detention Center, I couldn't get comfortable and I couldn't sleep. I took out my pocket-sized notebook, hoping to process some of what my eyes had seen. Nothing would come. As I put my pen to my notebook, the words I wrote were cuss words. Big, bold, bubble-letter cuss words. I wondered what the guy sitting next to me thought. But I couldn't stop coloring in the letters. When I told my friend Craig Stewart, confessing my shame over what had come out, he said, "I think that may be more biblical than we were raised to believe: a solid form of lament."

Craig knew Julia's story from the beginning, and although he lived far away, he closely monitored and encouraged my heart throughout the journey. He knew how tough the trip to the border was for me, and he'd been learning how to sit with pain with no agenda and no checklist. We often talked about lament and about learning to sit with the pain of others. Craig's post on Medium—a social media site— struck me deeply:

> Doubting Thomas has been ushering me to confront wounds and realities that I have avoided. Wounds and realities that are in turn helping me understand what it means to be white in South Africa at this time and place. To understand what it might mean to confront the wounds and pain that exist in this context. To recognize that truly working and yearning for resurrection means being willing to embrace and experience this pain which, in my place and time, is primarily the pain of black people, most especially black women.
>
> Dare I believe that if I am willing to see, touch, and experience the deepest death creating wounds in my life, community, and society they might actually lead me to discover resurrection? Thomas guides me to the truth that we can know the experience of death-defying resurrection hope, primarily when we are willing to confront the death and the wounds that caused it. Thomas does this, not with faith-filled bravado, but with doubt and anxiety, mirroring my emotions when confronting them.[13]

Craig showed me that I approached Thomas the disciple from a pedestal. I felt I was better than him. But seeing Thomas from my humanity gave me space to cuss, space to beg for healing, space to be anxious about the God I may find on the other side of deep lament.

As Soong-Chan Rah wrote in his book *Prophetic Lament,* "No amount of scriptural twisting can justify the brutal treatment of human beings made in the image of God."[14]

Human beings who have committed no criminal act are sitting in metal cages at Ursula and in glass-windowed cement cells at Port Isabel. When I visited Port Isabel, I met Jovita, dressed in a navy-blue prison uniform. She was ripped from her ten-year home in Alabama in an ICE raid. In front of her six- and eight-year-old American daughters, she was handcuffed and taken away. Her husband was away at work. When I met her at Port Isabel, she had been away from her family for one year.

After returning to her home in Central America, she waited nine months. Her husband paid a smuggler $1,500 US dollars to guide her by telephone up through Mexico. She never met the smuggler but called him at different intervals along the route to get her next set of directions.

"Were you scared?" my friend Tess asked her.

"Yes, very. I was all alone and I didn't know the route." Tears fell down her face as Jovita told us that her eight-year-old daughter had since tried to commit suicide, in constant fear that ICE will come for her father in the same way, and the two girls will be without both parents.

When Jovita talks on the phone with her younger daughter, the girl repeatedly asks, "Why did the police take you? When are you coming home?"

Jovita feels she has abandoned her children. She told us, "I feel like a bad mother." With tears streaming down my face, I looked into Jovita's eyes and told her with a resoluteness that steadied my voice, "You are a good mom. You are brave. We are proud of you, and we would do the exact same thing if we were torn from our children. You are a good mom."

It was impossible not to be emotional. There was no place where one could escape the feeling of being in jail—even in the barber shop. Above the four black barber chairs sitting in front of a long mirror were large orange letters: PORT ISABEL DETENTION CENTER. The water tower outside the center loomed over the caged soccer fields, the recreation center, the mess hall, the dormitory, and the medical clinic. On it was written "Immigration and Customs Enforcement" in huge letters, like a giant looking down and reminding the detainees that the American dream was certainly not for them.

In *Prophetic Lament,* Rah wrote, "Neither the absence of human comfort nor the human attempt to diffuse and minimize the emotional response of lament serves the suffering other. It only adds to the suffering."[15] Lament might look like cuss words that are wrong and shameful, because human suffering is wrong and shameful. Lament might look like a constant flow of tears, an inability to get out of bed, an angry rant, an emotional prayer. Lament might look like an acrostic of sadness, like this one I wrote for immigrants in response to anti-immigrant policy changes in 2017

I am lamenting the way the dominant culture—myself included —has acted toward Christ the Immigrant. How long, oh God, will You let the dominant culture continue:

Allowing the empire-mindset to determine how they treat you, acting as if you have less dignity, less inherent value, and less to offer the corporal body of the American church.

Burdening you with their burdens and silencing you when you speak about yours.

Conforming their churches to the nation's dominant culture rather than creating a better culture within the church that highlights your voice and intentionally seeks out the gifts you have.

Dehumanizing you, your struggle, your experience, and your spirit in word and deed and often, more strongly, in lack thereof.

Emancipating themselves and those who look like them before they seek to emancipate you.

Forgetting that many of their ancestors were immigrants, silencing those stories, and therefore numbing themselves to the hard realities of immigration. Forgetting that many of their ancestors oppressed Native Americans and African Americans despite fleeing their homelands because of oppression.

Gathering in spaces that are comfortable to them rather than entering into your home and, therefore, your life.

Hearing you but rarely listening.

Influencing you to think that the American dream is what everyone should strive for, and that their way of capitalism is the best solution to any country's woes.

Justifying their outrage over you "taking American jobs"—a euphemism for their laziness or worse, their own belief in the American prosperity gospel—yet never trying to understand the story that brought you to their soil, the toil it has taken and continues to take on your heart, soul, mind, and strength.

Kneeling to pray on the National Day of Prayer but failing to stand up to the powers that try to rob you of your dignity.

Listening without partnering, and failing to see you as a great teacher who has much to teach them.

Misguiding themselves into thinking that when they've heard one immigrant's story, they've heard them all.

Negating you as their neighbor, and thinking of you only in documentation statuses.

Organizing to protest against abortion through marches and votes, but failing to leave their houses or call their senators when your livelihood and life is in the fire.

Possessing their dominant language so much so that they look down on your accent, require you to speak with an American accent to fit in, gain employment, find housing, and fail to grasp the advanced education it requires to speak more than one language.

Questioning where your loyalties actually lie when American patriotism is at stake.

Restricting your upward movement within church leadership in predominantly white spaces.

Supporting their sent-out missionaries and placing them in high regard without considering the idea that you may be a missionary sent to them, with a keen awareness of their inherent cultural blind spots and spiritual weaknesses . . . and negating that their spiritual health increases when they are in good relationship with you.

Tokenizing you and those like you.

Undermining your ability to call two places home, overlooking the human difficulty this truly poses, and ignoring the spiritual maturity it gives you in light of eternity.

Viewing you as a demographic and/or financial gain in their church rather than mentors, leaders, and important bridges between people groups for the flourishing of the gospel.

Worshipping as individuals because their American culture idolizes independence, rather than learning from you of the richness of community and learning how to worship communally using collective pronouns rather than I, me, mine.

Xeroxing the stereotypes that their American culture has determined define your culture and projecting them onto you, so that whether you like the characteristics of that stereotype or not, you frequently feel you have to prove you are more than a stereotype.

Yielding to the spirit of White Supremacy in ways they are aware and unaware of, both in subtle and outright actions or lack thereof, in not recognizing that what they call "normal" is often normal for people whose skin tone, résumés, and bank accounts look similar to theirs, and not placing themselves in spaces where they are the minority enough to even glimpse what you deal with daily.

Zigzagging their way around the truth of their own cultural infirmities, inherited iniquities, and current responsibilities for the economic and spiritual glass ceilings they've encased above you.

Christ who comes as Stranger to welcome the stranger, hear our prayer and comfort those who suffer much at the hand of immigration enforcement, prejudice, and abuse, and cause those of us who don't suffer to be righteously burdened to enter into the suffering of our immigrant neighbors, brothers, and sisters. Lord, hear our prayer.[16]

Lament is a biblical discipline that we often ignore in white evangelicalism. Those of us in the dominant culture need to lean into lament, to learn from our brothers and sister of color, and to be fearless when the injustices around us that daily affect them create an ugly emotional response. We have an affinity for all things beautiful and Instagram-able in the white church. This idol denies us the ability to walk with others through suffering.

In a discussion with my friend Pastor Gricel Medina, she described this issue well.

We are promoting perfectionism, and perfectionism is counterproductive. The only perfect one is God. The stories of people are not pretty, but yet the church says just tell us the pretty stories. Do you see the oxymoron there? The church tells women to tell the pretty stories, because when you tell us the ugly stories, you make us feel uncomfortable. But you don't have any way or any right to rewrite my history so that you can be comfortable. Crying is not pretty. We need to let people cry. And no, it's not going to be pretty, but it'll be healing, and it'll be restoring. We're teaching our young women that you have to be strong and fierce all the time. And I believe in strong and fierce. I am strong and fierce, but not all the time. There are times I need a shoulder. . . . I need to be able to release the suffering and the pain and the things that I can't change. I have three women that have stage IV cancer; it's not pretty. I don't have an answer for them. All I can do is walk with them and hear their story.[17]

GET INVOLVED

Become friends with immigrants. If you take only one action step, this should be the one. I don't believe we should be motivated to act out of charity but rather out of biblical justice. The Old Testament lays out two important Hebrew words that help us understand what justice is. *Mishpat* is giving others what is due them, and *tsedaqah* is a life of right relationship. To base our advocacy work on a foundation that will stand, we must have relationships with those we are advocating for.

Adam Estle, director of Field and Constituencies at the National Immigration Forum, said,

I want Americans to understand the human realities that have led to the decisions people have made: either to send their children unaccompanied or to cross without authorization. When we think of the topic of immigration, it's easy to become polarized. But for Christians, once we think about immigrants as human beings created in the image of God, that changes everything. Building relationships with immigrants will lead people to be more welcoming not only at the interpersonal level, but also on a national level. The way I got into this work was through our church beginning to serve more and more immigrants who were coming through our doors, and in doing so we realized the avenues of assistance for them were very limited because of our broken laws. Our advocacy was motivated by trying to help others. People's minds are open to learn and have their assumptions challenged when they are motivated by relationships.[18]

According to LifeWay Research, 21 percent of evangelical Christians say they have been encouraged by their local church to reach out to immigrants in their community. Additionally, the most effective influence that evangelicals have in determining their personal immigration philosophy is the immigrants they've interacted with.[19]

Foster unaccompanied minors. Some foster parents become licensed in order to foster unaccompanied minors. Adam, who you heard from above, lives in Peoria, Arizona, a suburb of Phoenix. From 2014 to 2015, he helped run a school designed for unaccompanied minors, funded by an emergency grant. At night and on weekends, the children went back to their foster families. He said,

> The maximum capacity we had was for fourteen kids, and they ranged in age from three to twelve. Our family was one of the foster families for the program until the Office of Refugee Resettlement said that it was a conflict of interest for me to run the program and be a foster parent. We had a ten-year-old from Guatemala living with us at the time who we had to move to another home. When the program ended—it was funded only as an emergency response and in 2015, it was no longer deemed a crisis by the US government—we transferred our foster license to Catholic Charities, which was also doing work locally, serving UACs [unaccompanied alien children]. Soon thereafter, we had a nine-year-old boy come to live with us from Honduras.

Adam said that although he was well-versed in immigration policy, he and his wife were surprised at what they saw in this specific circumstance.

> We got into this thinking that a minor wouldn't end up in long-term foster care unless he or she has no one and nowhere else to

go, but we found out quickly that his mom was still in the picture, back in Honduras. Our minor didn't have a dad, so it was easy for me to fill that role and bond well with him. But it was really hard for my wife to be a mother figure, because he already had a mom and was talking to her every week.

Though the boy no longer lives with his family, Adam remains involved in immigration issues.

I work for an immigration advocacy organization, and I'm having high-level policy conversations about the UAC program, so the experience of having that role of a national advocate while having a UAC actually living in our home was really interesting. I think it is really easy when working on national immigration policy and advocacy to lose sight of the human reality of what is happening on the ground. I'm really grateful I've been able to keep my family in Arizona and be in a community where these policies are affecting my neighbors. [The boy] was in our home when the 2016 election happened, and my biological kids were asking, "Is the government going to come into our home and take him?" This whole experience took the theoretical concerns and made them real for me on a personal level.[20]

Volunteer, give, research. Many organizations are doing immigration and foster-care advocacy work. Here are a few:

- Bethany Christian Services
- Catholic Charities
- Department of Health and Human Services (your local office for foster care)
- The Door (New York City)
- Evangelical Immigration Table
- The Immigration Project

- Justice for Immigrants (US Catholic Bishops Campaign)
- Justice in Motion
- Kids in Need of Defense (KIND) (there are local law offices all around the country that do this on a smaller scale)
- Lutheran Immigration and Refugee Services
- Immigration Advocates Network
- Interfaith Immigration Coalition
- Migration Policy Institute
- National Immigration Forum
- Pew Hispanic Center
- RAICES
- Refugee Council US
- El Refugio Ministry
- United States Conference of Catholic Bishops
- We Welcome Refugees
- World Relief

Read books. The following are a few books to read that speak specifically to the issues addressed in this book: immigration, family separation, undocumented immigration, border policy, and foster care.

- *Christians at the Border*, M. Daniel Carroll R.
- *The Distance Between Us*, Reyna Grande
- *Enrique's Journey*, Sonia Nazario
- *The God Who Sees*, Karen González
- *In the Country We Love: My Family Divided*, Diane Guerrero
- *The Line Becomes a River*, Francisco Cantú
- *Love Undocumented*, Sarah Quezada

- *Lucky Boy*, Shanthi Sekaran

- *Tell Me How It Ends*, Valeria Luiselli

- *Three Little Words*, Ashley Rhodes-Courter

- *To the End of June*, Cris Beam

- *Welcoming the Stranger*, Matthew Soerens and Jenny Yang

Speak to your elected officials. Matthew Soerens and Jenny Yang's book, *Welcoming the Stranger*, offers a plethora of resources on how to get involved. I highly recommend reading the book and accessing its wealth of information. In appendix five, the authors advise on contacting representatives:

> Contacting your elected official is easy. The first step is to know who they are. Each citizen of the United States is represented in Washington by one representative, who represents a congressional district, and by two senators, who each represent the entire state. To find your representative and senators, call the congressional switchboard at 202-224-3121 or check online at house.gov and senate.gov. To contact the White House, visit whitehouse.gov. World Relief also has online tools to determine which elected officials represent you and to send them an email message at worldrelief.org/advocate.
>
> When you call, state your name, where you are calling from, and then express your opinion. If there is a particular bill that you would like your elected representative to support or not support, be sure to mention the bill name or number.[21]

The appendix of *Welcoming the Stranger* includes what to do when writing a letter or an email.

A FORSAKING FATHER

In the Bodega, Lupe's captors, wondering if she was dead, threw cold water on her. "God, why have you forgotten me?" she asked.

"We are your god now," the captors responded.

On the cross, below a sign written by his mockers that said, "King of the Jews," Jesus asked a similar question of his Father: "From noon until three in the afternoon darkness came over all the land. About three in the afternoon Jesus cried out in a loud voice, '*Eli, Eli, lema sabachthani?*' (which means 'My God, my God, why have you forsaken me?')" (Matthew 27:45-46).

Lupe's story has a way of pushing me to the edges of my doubt. Why did God forsake her on her journey north? Why does God forsake so many who make the same journey? Sometimes I don't want to lament. I don't want to pray. I don't want anything to do with spiritual disciplines because I don't want to talk to a God who forsakes people. There are moments when I want to flip over whatever table God is sitting at. There are moments that the brokenness is too overwhelming, too sickening, too frightening.

I want revenge on the people that harmed Lupe and Julia. Revenge on the messed-up systems. Revenge on the politicians who are completely out of touch with the humanity that's broken by the decisions they make. Revenge on the drug cartels that see humans as economic pawns and nothing more. When humanity is truncated, when human beings are dehumanized, the question persists: has God forsaken us?

Like Jesus, when darkness overtakes us, we cry out, "Why, God? Why have you forsaken us? How long, oh Lord?"

I could write many already-argued answers to this question. I could talk about God's permissible will and his perfect will. I could say that the brokenness of this world is meant to be patched up by broken humans, who recognize their own brokenness in the process of healing each other's wounds. I could say that the people of God were always meant to carry each other's burdens, to learn to truly live in community, to empathize authentically. I could—and I will—say that we must learn to stop dehumanizing each other in language and in actions, and that we can advocate for Lupe and those like her by getting involved politically.

But in the valley of the shadow of death, the above answers won't do. In the valley, we must reach out for the one comfort Christ gives us in the shadow of his own death. When we scream at God, "Where are you?" we are, in fact, imitating Christ. We are practicing a spiritual discipline that Christ, fully God and fully man, gave us. Our humanity and our divinity have collided. In these moments, the thin places of this world are created, and heaven and earth intertwine.

The messiah we would have never chosen in our own humanity—the vulnerable, outcast weirdo who rides donkeys and wears no armor—is the messiah our humanity desperately needs, the One who not only empathizes with suffering but also has a long personal and familial history of it.

Pastor Gricel's statement that she doesn't have an answer for her three friends with stage IV cancer is a humble pastoral admission. Our Christian culture tells pastors they must have all the answers. And our Christian culture tells believers we should never doubt our faith. Yet authenticity makes room for doubt.

I don't know how to answer my own doubts about God and suffering. I really don't. But as writer Jonathan Merritt says, the phrase "I don't know" is holy.[22] Sometimes getting over the fear of asking certain questions is just as important as any answer we may find. If Jesus can ask what feels like a heretical question to God, who is omnipresent, then we can too. God isn't scared of our humanity; we shouldn't be, either.

UPDATES ON OUR LIVES

A few months after Julia moved home to Honduras, my family and I moved from North Carolina to Tennessee. Andrew and I celebrated our tenth anniversary by going to eat hibachi chicken and sushi with our children a few miles from our new home. The tropical-fish tank in the restaurant held wonder for our little Juniper. We also had a full-blown discussion with Cade about whether or not to purchase a pair of the trainer chopsticks he saw hanging on the wall for sale. He's serious about learning to eat with them.

Foster licenses do not transfer between states, so for now, we're taking a break from fostering, unsure how long it will last. As we settle into a new phase of life, we remain in constant contact with Lupe, Julia, Enrique, Fernando, and Samuel. When I was applying for the job in Tennessee, Lupe was praying for me. When I told her about how we were struggling with the decision to move because we'd be moving away from family, she offered solid counsel. She also kept me levelheaded when family tensions rose over the potential move. After a particularly frustrating interaction with family, she gave me this good counsel: "They love you so much, Gena. They are upset because of their love."

Likewise, when Lupe interviewed for a new job in San Pedro Sula, I was praying for her. We rejoiced together when we landed our new jobs. We check up on each other, sending pictures and voice messages.

In February 2019, Julia started elementary school in Honduras. Simultaneously, news emerged in the United States that thousands more families had been separated prior to the announcement of the zero-tolerance policy in April 2018. The total number at the time was unknown, according to a report by the Office of Inspector General.[23] While Julia was able to reunite with her family, many children who've been separated may not be. Some days I read this news and stay informed without any repercussions; other days its weight was too much for me to maintain physical composure. I cried. I wailed. I fell to the ground. I felt depressed. I started seeing a therapist.

SPEAKING UP

When Andrew and I hear dehumanizing speech about immigrants, whether from family, friends, or strangers, we speak up. That boldness comes from our relationships *and* intangible conviction. When I hear Christians get defensive about homes and jobs, I try to point the conversation back to Christ, because Lupe pointed me to Christ.

Jesus' story of the good Samaritan (Luke 10) breaks down our justifications for maintaining the status quo in how we approach others. Can we see a Honduran immigrant as the good Samaritan? Can we see ourselves as the Levite in the story? Our responses to the moral questions Christ's parables pose reveal much about us as individuals. What do we do with Jesus' radical story, which affirms his revolutionary teaching of love for enemies? And just as importantly, whose enemy are we?

For better or worse, Christianity is known by its relationships— amity and enmity—with others. The issue of immigration is bigger than politics; it's about relationships.

As author Michael Wear said,

Christians are obliged to work for the benefit and flourishing of all people whether or not they see the world as we do or agree with us in any way. A Christian's obligation is not to their tribe, but to their God. . . . The crisis for Christians is not that we are politically homeless, the crisis is that we ever thought we could make our home in politics at all. Our home is with Him who has made His home in us and our hope is in the kingdom that is right at hand. . . . Christians go to politics to advance justice and affirm dignity. We get our emotional and spiritual needs met elsewhere.[24]

What would it look like if we worked for the benefit and flourishing of immigrants, whether or not they see the world as we do or agree with us in any way? What would it look like if we stopped forming political tribes of Christianity and involved ourselves in politics solely to advance justice and affirm dignity?

THE MOTHER LOVE OF GOD

The God who birthed Julia, Emma, and Karen is the same God who birthed me, my Republican friends, my Democrat friends, and my biological children. God has birthed those who fit my idea of the right type of Christians. He has birthed those who fit my idea of the wrong type of Christians.[25] He breathes life into the unaccompanied and the accompanied, the abandoned and the cared-for, the neglected, widows, widowers, successful businesspeople, pastors, priests, and faithful and unfaithful congregants.

God—whom I've long known as Forgiving Father—I now also see as Inclusive Mother. God births life and cares about every child's needs. Like Lupe, who risked the wrath of the coyotes to miraculously breastfeed a child not her own, God risks and sacrifices to bring us all into her everlasting nourishment.

In the relentless love of Lupe, I saw the tenacity and power of God's abundant love that disregards boundaries and labels. Indeed, there is no border that can separate us from the mother love of God.

EPILOGUE

DEAR JULIA

As I write this, Julia, you are five years old. By the time this book is published, you'll be seven. You may never read it, and that's okay. One day, if you do read it, I hope you will think I have shared your story well. You might be mad I've shared it, and I wouldn't blame you. After all, it's your story more than it is mine. I pray you'll believe in the good that can and will come from sharing it. Your mom and I made a lot of decisions without your consent when writing this story. Had you been a teenager, we would have discussed these with you.

Yesterday you asked me if I could send your bicycle from my house in the United States to your house in Honduras. You were upset when I told you that I can't. I hope the remainder of your childhood contains only childlike worries like this, and I'm glad this is the heaviest issue on your heart right now.

Thank you, Julia, for letting me and my family be a part of your story. The imprint you and your family have made on our hearts will last a lifetime. I look forward to watching you grow up, even from afar. I'm confident we will meet again and again. I love you to the moon and back.

ACKNOWLEDGMENTS

Without a doubt, books are created in community. This book is the product of many of my typically separate communities coming together.

Andrew: thank you for saying yes to the social worker. Thank you for your hard work, constant love, and willingness to be stretched with me. Thank you for your honesty, accountability, and sacrifice, not only in being a foster dad but also in being married to a writer. I love you. Thank you for being my safe space, and giving me space to grieve and grow. Thank you for your understanding in the midst of my brokenness. *Eres mi media naranja.*

Cademon and Juniper: thank you for your willingness to love others while being stretched by decisions you didn't make. I'm so proud of each of you in immeasurable ways. Thank you for constantly teaching me so much about life and love and goodness. Cade, thank you for letting me share stories about you. Your vulnerability and strength continue to amaze me. You are a wise warrior indeed.

Emma and Karen: thank you for being a part of our family, even if only for a little while. You both left lasting impressions on my heart and on my life.

Alan and Tina Smith, and George and Belinda Thomas: thank you. You are the best grandparents any kid could ever ask for, and you loved Julia so well. Thank you for being our respite at the drop of a hat when we desperately needed it. Andrew and I are forever in your debt. Like you always say, Pops, I owe you my life!

Antoine Lassiter: thank you for your spiritual leadership and for sharing from your background in foster care, which proved so helpful at such a critical time. I'm grateful for the countercultural ways in which you live and lead those around you.

Mission 217 folks, especially Antoine and Tonia Lassiter, Steve and Leah Parish, Sweet Peak, Gary Wyrick, Bruce and Penny Heglar, Tiffany Lassiter, Amanda Boone, Yve Pringle, Debi Wright, and Bridgette Benton, who leaned in and loved Julia: it was such a blessing to see Julia accepted and loved in the many ways she was by each of you. And to Sarah Causey for sharing your expertise and reminding me to take care of myself.

Cory and Nathalia Lewis, Aaron and Jenna Thomas, Luke and Amy Lunceford, Lashonda Houston, and Minda Searcy: thank you for loving Julia as you did.

The social workers and supervisors at my local social services office: thank you! You never get the credit you deserve, and I wish you would let me list your names here. Nonetheless, thank you for fighting alongside me as best you could to get Julia home. I'm so proud of our community and all the efforts made to get her back into Lupe's arms. Thank you for the work you do for the children of our county, and thanks to your families for all they sacrifice so you can do such work.

My local fostering community: thank you for all the love and support you have given me and my family, especially Norma and Scott for your love for Julia, and Amber and Brenda for all you do to support all of us.

Ms. Katrina and Ms. Adrienne and the other staff at Julia's preschool: we are confident your loving educational environment was a catalyst in many positive outcomes of Julia's behavior and language learning. I'll never stop singing your praises.

Craig Stewart and Lisa Collier: thank you for loving and encouraging me throughout this whole process from afar. I am very grateful for your presence in my life. I also thank God for WhatsApp.

Laurel Fiorelli: thank you for your honest encouragement and embodiment of the gospel. From the moment we met, you have not stopped amazing me, inspiring me, and encouraging me in immeasurable ways.

Michael Jimenez: thank you for prompting me to read Valeria Luiselli's *Tell Me How It Ends*, which proved to be an invaluable resource for me. Also thanks for suggesting Francisco Cantú's *The Line Becomes a River*. I'm grateful to be connected to you and encouraged by you.

Thank you, Carolina Hinojosa-Cisneros, for suggesting Shanthi Sekaran's *Lucky Boy* and for leading me to Ada María Isasi-Díaz's *Mujerista Theology*, and for your own beautiful poetry, especially *Blessed Be the Mother*. You challenge me to be a better writer. I'm grateful we are friends, and I'm amazed at the beautiful gift of writing you've been given and have so graciously given the rest of us.

Kathy Khang: thank you for risking in the ways you do to give others a platform. Thank you for teaching me by example to raise my voice.

Ryan Kuja: thanks for lending an ear and giving me sage advice when I needed it.

Michael Gaspeny (Dr. G): thank you for refining this craft of writing within me all those years ago. You remain one of my most favorite people in this world.

Allan F.: thank you for translating chapters back into Spanish so that Lupe could read them. Finding the right translator with such a delicate story was so important and I'm ever grateful.

Anna Fargo: thank you for telling me to write this book long before I had plans to do so. Your constant concern for Julia and other children being torn from their parents at the border gave me necessary hope at a difficult time.

Al Hsu: thank you for working through this manuscript with me and for your valuable insight, both on the page and beyond.

Elí Romero: thank you for answering my questions and allowing me to tell part of your immigration story and to talk about your beautiful mother. I'm grateful for your voice and life in this world. You make this country a better place by being here, *paisano*. I await your future articles and books with great anticipation!

Michelle Warren and Cathleen Farrell, along with the wonderful folks at the National Immigration Forum: thank you for allowing me to see the processing and detention facilities in McAllen, Texas. And thank you, Jennifer Podkul and Christian Penichet-Paul, for answering my bazillion questions about immigration. Words cannot express how impactful that trip was at such a critical time. And for my fellow comrades on the trip—Tess Clarke, Kathryn Freeman, Alexandra Kuykendall, Carol Kuykendall, Sarah Quezada, Vickie Reddy, and Meghan Smith—thank you for letting me learn with and through you.

And finally, thank you, Lupe, for entrusting your story to me. You are braver than any woman I know, and I am beyond privileged to call you friend.

A NOTE TO OTHER FOSTER PARENTS

Immigration is not far removed from foster care and adoption. And immigrants tend to have a deeper understanding of what foster children go through. They must learn the geography of another land, the de facto and de jure laws of said land, the visible and invisible culture of the people, and the basics of the language. On a smaller scale, foster children (and adoptees) must learn the lay of the home, the de facto and de jure rules of the home, the visible and invisible culture of the family, and the basics of the language used in the home.

As I write this, it's unclear how many of the zero-tolerance policy victims have been placed in foster care. Julia was both an immigrant in a land not her own and an immigrant in a home not her own.

For those of us who foster, it does us good to research culture shock, assimilation, and reverse culture shock (most felt when children go to parent meetings and then come back into the foster home) as a way of better understanding one of the many layers of this process.[1]

Most professionals I talked to about our case had no idea what we needed to do. I hope you might use this information to figure out what you need to do. Note that the following assumes the biological parents are back in their home country.

Make contact (and stay in contact) with the biological family. During the first two weeks of Julia being in our home, we didn't know where her mom was. We finally got Lupe's contact information from our social worker, who got it from the sponsorship family, I believe. It was immediately clear from the first video chat that we had the right person. Julia was emotional, excited, and clearly familiar with her mom's face.

Get the child into therapy, if possible. Advocate for the right therapist. It was a struggle to find a therapist in our area who spoke Spanish. After finding one, it was clear she didn't see the issues we were seeing. Deep conversations about trauma and hurt require better Spanish than I can speak, and watching the therapist struggle to have simple conversations with Julia made us realize she was not the best fit. Unfortunately we didn't find another before Julia went back to Honduras.

Make contact with the consulate. We attempted to contact the Honduran equivalent of our Department of Health and Human Services (DHHS) first, but that didn't get us very far. Contacting the Honduran consulate—after taking some time to figure out which one had jurisdiction over our region—was the best thing we did. Ultimately, the Honduran Consulate was responsible for administering the travel papers we needed for Julia to return home; she couldn't leave the United States without those papers, since she didn't have a passport. Also note that email and texts worked better than phone calls.

Get a home study done. This is necessary in typical DHHS court proceedings, as a judge won't rule for reunification without knowing the home is safe and appropriate for the child. (I tried finding a loophole but could not.) The Honduran consulate was able to work with Dirección de Niñez, Adolescencia y Familia (DINAF) to get a home study done for Lupe. If the consulate you work with can't do one, there is likely a private agency that can.

Attend court as much as possible. This keeps you in the loop of what's happening with your case and shows the lawyers and the judge that you're active and interested.

Use the home study at adjudication, if possible. At Julia's adjudication, we were able to have Lupe testify through WhatsApp and a translator. We also gave the judge the home-study results, with hopes that the he would rule in favor of reunification. He did.

Continue to work with the consulate to get the required travel documents so the unaccompanied minor can return home to his or her parents. We had to wait about two months for all the paperwork to be completed by the judge in order for the consulate to give us the travel papers we needed. Keep in mind that for all of the paperwork to be filled out, the biological parents spend money in their own country to get the legal paperwork notarized. They may even require the services of a lawyer.

Travel with the child. If needed, advocate to do this. I was adamant that I wanted to travel with Julia back to her home, because I didn't want her traveling with someone she didn't know. She had already been through enough trauma.

AN INTERVIEW WITH ELÍ ROMERO

María, the mother of my longtime friend Elí, died in early 2018, more than a decade after we'd met. She had owned a little business selling clothes, fabrics, and dishware at an indoor market. At the time, Elí had been living in the United States for a few years after arriving on a travel visa that he overstayed. If he had attended María's funeral, he would have risked losing his job and his home. I wondered, How many others have had to mourn the loss of their loved ones from thousands of miles away because acquiring travel papers is a privilege they don't possess? In late fall of 2018, I interviewed Elí about his mother and life in the United States.

I could tell you so many good things my mom did," he said. "But when I remember her, I think about this one day that we were sitting in the market stall. We were talking, sitting, and drinking coffee. She told me I should continue her work of helping others and telling those who don't know God about him. She lived trying to take the Word of God to everyone she visited with. I've never seen a spark in anyone's eyes quite like the one I saw in my mom's when she would visit the sick or bring food to the senior citizens at the community house, or when she brought food to people in jail and talked to them about love, forgiveness, and the mercy of God. She loved doing this work because the most important thing to her was to fulfill the Holy Scriptures."

I asked, "When your mom died, how did you feel knowing you couldn't be with the rest of your family?"

"The day I left Honduras, my mother said to me, 'Son, work hard, always ask for guidance from God, behave well, and honor everything I have taught you.' In the depths of both of our hearts we knew it would be our final goodbye. When we talked on video chat, she told me that she prayed for me every day and that I always had her support."

Before María died, Elí had more than a feeling foretelling her death. "I had a vision that she came to me and said goodbye. She entered my bedroom and sat on the edge of my bed as I lay there. She asked me, 'How are you?' and I said, 'I'm well,' but I felt surprised. Her hair was totally black—without one white hair. Her skin didn't have any splotches on it, and her mouth and her eyes were radiating happiness. She told me she was going to be fine and that I didn't need to worry at all. She told me not to look back and to work hard to pay for my house. She was dressed like she always was, with a knee-length skirt and a polyester blouse. From her pocket, she took out a rosary and told me to wear it on my neck and pray to the Virgin Mary like she taught me. Before she left my room, she gave me a blessing and repeated that I didn't need to look back or move back to Honduras, but that everything would be okay.

"A few hours later, around midday in Honduras, my brother called me and told me that my mom was at the clinic and could not speak but could listen and react to voices. So I began talking to her. As soon as she heard my voice, she said with a great hardship, 'Negrito, is that you?' I told her I loved her and a million more things. At the end, I sang her a part of her favorite song, 'Cipota de Barrio':

> Reina de la lluvia
> Dueña de los charcos
> Si te da la gana
> Mamá de muñecas
> amiga de pájaros
> sapos y ranas.

Cipota traviesa
Patoja de mi alma
Sandía y melón,
Semilla de patria
La pájara pinta
En un verde limón.[1]

"I could hear her smile, and she said, 'I love you.'"

An hour later, Elí was sitting at a table, trying to eat his lunch. "A wave of anguish came over me like I've never felt before. All of the sudden, a profound sadness filled my chest, and I felt an enormous emptiness in my stomach. I wanted to cry, but I couldn't. The only thing I could do was stay put and look out at nothing. At that moment, I heard my mom say, 'Everything is going to be fine, Negrito.'

"By the time my brother called to tell me she had passed away, I already knew. Not being able to be there for her wake and her funeral represents a disheartening pain unlike any other I've ever had."

I asked Elí if he knew when he left for the United States that he'd miss special occasions in the lives of his family members.

"Yes. Without a doubt," he replied. "A caress in the right moment has more value than a million words from a distance. To see photographs or be on video calls, watching my children grow, watching them get more beautiful, more creative—or to see my family come together for holiday meals—reminds me constantly that distance favors sadness. It is profoundly sad to not be near my family or near my daughters. That is the truth."

"So why risk coming to the United States, or why risk staying?" I asked.

"According to the laws of this country, we are called illegals. But this refers to the laws of North Americans that we are considered illegal. But I don't believe it's illegal to work for the health and benefit of your family. It's not illegal if your job gives a boost to the American economy. It is not illegal to try to work to the best of your ability in this country that has the opportunity and capacity that our home countries do not possess. Many, many of us who are undocumented are here searching for a future of better probabilities, probabilities that in our own countries were negated principally because of corrupt governments. And that is precisely why delinquency grows—because of corruption. I don't feel happy that my daughters live in a place with corrupt police, corrupt justice systems, and a corrupt government. The social risks for my family of me being here are gigantic. But like my mother taught me, I pray for my family and families in general, that nothing bad or sad will happen to them."

I asked, "What regrets do you have in the process of coming here to the United States?"

"My mother and I had a special bond that was different between us than what she had with my siblings. For forty-five years, she had her business at the market stall. Of that time, I spent fifteen years there with her helping her with sales and everything else, and during those years, we had thousands of talks where she would advise me or tell me stories of her life. Her life was an example. She was born and grew up very poor. But, later in life, she lived as though she was a millionaire, because she reaped what she sowed. I saw her interact with many different people who came to our business, and she would give them corn, rice, beans, yucca, bananas, or other necessities for free. If someone gave her something for free, she'd share with others who needed it more. She told me, 'Son, life is about sharing. Don't give what you have leftover; rather, share what you have now.' I don't have any regrets with my mom, but rather with myself because I feel that I have failed in the homework she gave me: to help those in need. I do what I can, but I feel like it's not enough."

I asked my final question for Elí: "If you could change immigration laws, what would you change?"

"I think the United States is what it is precisely because of its laws. These laws are severe and disagreeable for undocumented immigrants.

I know that the president [Donald Trump] is famous for being cruel and even inhumane, and I believe that he will never understand the weight of the words *distance, sadness, persecution, threat, anxiety, depression, anguish,* because poverty was never something he experienced. What can I do? Sadly, not much. There are some pro-immigrant organizations that have managed to bring some benefits and help to undocumented immigrants. Right now, many of these organizations are being scrutinized by ICE. Every time something happens, we are more and more afraid to get near these organizations for the threat of being captured and deported."

He finished his thoughts with this: "If I could change one thing—for now, I just want them to stop separating families. The minimum suffering caused by this will be seismic damage. Separating parents from children [causes] tremendous and irreversible damage, specifically because the children's concept of love in human form—their parents—is ripped from them."

SMALL-GROUP
DISCUSSION QUESTIONS

1. In what ways do you see God pursuing Lupe throughout her life? Julia? Gena?

2. What life circumstances contributed to Lupe's decision to try to cross the border into the United States? If you were in her shoes, what would you have done to supply the family's economic needs?

3. What differences separated the lives of Lupe and Gena? Were there any similarities?

4. Can you imagine being separated from your child or family member whether by governmental force or by economic influences? What questions would you have for God if you were in such a situation? How do you think that separation would affect your faith?

5. What do you think are some of the most difficult aspects of foster care? What do you think are some of the most beautiful?

6. Imagine yourself as a child suddenly having to move to another home to be with another family. What fears would you have?

7. Julia struggled with her skin color but was able to see herself differently when other Christians of her same skin tone told her she was beautiful. Why was living in a multiracial community important for her? Is it important for you? Why or why not?

8. Share a time when you were baptized and came into a fuller understanding of God's goodness, whether a physical baptism or the baptism of a life event.

9. How do you think Christians should respond to immigration? Have your views been changed by Julia's story?

10. Do you believe that God is neither male nor female? What aspects of a mother's love are left out when we speak of God only as Father?

11. Do you think God cares about labels? Are labels helpful to understand life better? Do they promote exclusivity?

12. Do you know any foster parents or immigrant parents? How can you better support and encourage them?

NOTES

FOREWORD

[1]American Immigration Council, "U.S. Citizen Children Impacted by Immigration Enforcement," May 23, 2018, www.americanimmigrationcouncil.org/research/us-citizen-children-impacted-immigration-enforcement.

INTRODUCTION

[1]United States Department of Justice, "Attorney General Announces Zero-Tolerance Policy for Criminal Illegal Entry," April 6, 2018, www.justice.gov/opa/pr/attorney-general-announces-zero-tolerance-policy-criminal-illegal-entry.

[2]As of January 2019, the total known number of separated children had reached 2,737, but "thousands more" were likely separated by the Trump administration. See *New York Times*, "Family Separation May Have Hit Thousands More Migrant Children Than Reported," www.nytimes.com/2019/01/17/us/family-separation-trump-administration-migrants.html.

[3]Tom Dart, "2,000 Children Separated from Parents in Six Weeks Under Trump Policy," *Guardian*, June 16, 2018, www.theguardian.com/us-news/2018/jun/16/children-separated-parents-border-trump-administration.

[4]Michelle Ferrigno Warren, *The Power of Proximity* (Downers Grove, IL: InterVarsity Press, 2017), 108.

1: *EMIGRACIÓN*

[1]Miles B. Lawrence, "Preliminary Report: Hurricane Lili," National Hurricane Center, November 18, 1996, web.archive.org/web/20100825052752/http://www.nhc.noaa.gov/1996lili.html.

[2]"The World Factbook: Honduras," CIA World Factbook, modified June 20, 2018, www.cia.gov/library/publications/the-world-factbook/geos/ho.html.

[3]"Honduras Country Profile," BBC News, May 16, 2018, www.bbc.com /news/world-latin-america-18954311.

[4]George Gao, "5 Facts about Honduras and Immigration," Pew Research, August 11, 2014, www.pewresearch.org/fact-tank/2014/08/11/5-facts-about -honduras-and-immigration/.

[5]Anuradha Seth, "Towards Human Resilience: Sustaining MDG Progress in an Age of Economic Uncertainty," UNDP, September 2011, www.undp .org/content/undp/en/home/librarypage/poverty-reduction/inclusive _development/towards_human_resiliencesustainingmdgprogressinanageof economicun.html.

[6]"The World Factbook: Honduras," CIA World Factbook, modified June 20, 2018, https://www.cia.gov/library/publications/resources/the-world-factbook /geos/ho.html.

[7]Bruce Horovitz, "Chiquita OKs $681M Sale to Brazil Bidders," *USA Today*, October 27, 2014, www.usatoday.com/story/money/business/2014/10/27 /chiquita-brazil-deal/17997003/.

[8]Allison Piper, "The Creation of a Banana Empire: An Investigation into the Chiquita Brand," *Harvard Political Review*, June 10, 2017, harvardpolitics .com/world/the-creation-of-a-banana-empire-an-investigation-into-chiquita -brand/.

[9]Marcelo Bucheli, "Good Dictator, Bad Dictator: United Fruit Company and Economic Nationalism in Central America in the Twentieth Century," 2006, business.illinois.edu/working_papers/papers/06-0115.pdf.

[10]Piper, "The Creation of a Banana Empire."

[11]Daniel Kurtz-Phelan, "Big Fruit," *New York Times*, March 2, 2008, www .nytimes.com/2008/03/02/books/review/Kurtz-Phelan-t.html.

[12]Delphine Schrank, "Fear, Solidarity Drive Migrants to Stick with Mexico 'Caravan,'" Reuters, April 5, 2018, www.reuters.com/article/us-usa-immigration -caravan/fear-solidarity-drive-migrants-to-stick-with-mexico-caravan -idUSKCN1HC2H9.

[13]Salil Shetty, "Most Dangerous Journey: What Central American Migrants Face When They Try to Cross the Border," Amnesty International, www .amnestyusa.org/most-dangerous-journey-what-central-american -migrants-face-when-they-try-to-cross-the-border/.

[14]SPLC, "Trump and His Troll Army Declare War on 'Caravan' of Migrants Fleeing Persecution," April 2, 2018, www.splcenter.org/hatewatch /2018/04/02/trump-and-his-troll-army-declare-war-caravan-migrants -fleeing-persecution.

[15]SPLC, "Trump and His Troll Army."

[16]Joshua Partlow and Nick Miroff, "For Central Americans, Children Open a Path to the U.S.—And Bring a Discount," *Washington Post*, November 23, 2018, www.washingtonpost.com/world/national-security/for-central-americans -children-open-a-path-to-the-us--and-bring-a-discount/2018/11/19/baf3b092 -e6ce-11e8-bbdb-72fdbf9d4fed_story.html?utm_term=.f1461ba1f782.

[17]Border Patrol Agents are under the banner of the federal law enforcement agency, Customs and Border Protection of the Department of Homeland Security. Border Patrol Agents, who wear green uniforms, are responsible for protecting the actual border of the United States. While Border Patrol Agents work closely with Customs and Border Patrol Officers (CBPO) they are not the same. CBPOs wear blue uniforms and work specifically at ports of entry.

[18]It's unclear what happened at the border with Carlos. The three scenarios listed all seem viable based on researching policies, combing through news reports, and talking with immigration officials. Between October 2017 and April 2018, more than seven hundred children were separated from their parents at the border prior to the zero-tolerance policy's announcement. See Caitlin Dickerson, "Hundreds of Immigrant Children Have Been Taken From Parents at U.S. Border," *New York Times*, April 20, 2018, www.nytimes .com/2018/04/20/us/immigrant-children-separation-ice.html. Additionally, in January 2019, new reports came out saying that separations were happening as early as June 2017. See also Miriam Jordan, "Family Separation May Have Hit Thousands More Migrant Children Than Reported," *New York Times*, January 17, 2019, www.nytimes.com/2019/01/17/us/family -separation-trump-administration-migrants.html. I was unable to find clear policy statements on when US Customs and Border Protection uses DNA tests. For more about the process in general, see the American Immigration Council's "Guide to Children Arriving at the Border: Laws, Policies and Responses," June 25, 2015, www.americanimmigrationcouncil.org/research /guide-children-arriving-border-laws-policies-and-responses.

2: EXPATRIATION

[1]Kieran Nash, "The Difference between an Expat and an Immigrant? Semantics," BBC, updated January 20, 2017, www.bbc.com/capital/story/2017 0119-who-should-be-called-an-expat.

[2]Online Etymology Dictionary, s.v. "expatriate," www.etymonline.com/word /expatriate.

[3]*Mara* can mean group of friends, gang, etc.

3: RÍO BRAVO

[1]UNESCO, Maya Site of Copan, everything-everywhere.com/unesco -world-heritage-site-194-maya-site-of-copan/.

[2]Shanthi Sekaran, *Lucky Boy* (New York: G. P. Putnam's Sons, 2016), 120.

[3]Oscar Lopez, "Mexican Police Probe Suspected Trafficking Along US-Mexico Border," Reuters, October 14, 2018, www.reuters.com/article/us -mexico-trafficking/mexican-police-probe-suspected-trafficking-along -u-s-mexico-border-idUSKCN1MO0B4.

[4]Jeffrey Hallock, Ariel G. Ruiz Soto, and Michael Fix, "In Search of Safety, Growing Numbers of Women Flee Central America," Migration Policy Institute, May 30, 2018, www.migrationpolicy.org/article/search-safety -growing-numbers-women-flee-central-america.

[5]Terry Frieden, "18 Human Cargo Deaths in Texas," CNN, May 14, 2003, www.cnn.com/2003/US/Southwest/05/14/truck.bodies/index.html.

[6]Kate Linthicum and Jenny Jarvie, "Migrants Trapped in Sweltering Truck in Texas Were 'Lying on the Floor Like Meat,' Driver Says," *Los Angeles Times*, July 24, 2017, www.latimes.com/nation/la-na-texas-migrant-deaths -20170724-story.html.

[7]María Sánchez Díez and Jessica Weiss, "'It's Out of a Horror Film': We asked Latinos Who Migrated to the U.S. in the Backs of Trucks to Share Their Stories," Univision, July 28, 2017, www.univision.com/univision-news /immigration/its-out-of-a-horror-film-we-asked-latinos-who-migrated -to-the-us-in-the-backs-of-trucks-to-share-their-stories.

[8]Francisco Cantú, *The Line Becomes a River* (New York: Riverhead Books, 2018), 93.

4: RIO GRANDE

[1]This number is inconsistent throughout this book because different sources have differing statistics. According to a 2019 *Washington Post* article, this 60 percent to 80 percent figure is not accurate. See Glenn Kessler, "No, Amnesty International Does Not Say 60 Percent of Migrant Women in Mexico Have Been Raped," *Washington Post*, February 1, 2019, www.washingtonpost.com /politics/2019/02/01/no-amnesty-international-does-not-say-percent -migrant-women-mexico-have-been-raped/?utm_term=.6b9e565c89f2.

[2]Valeria Luiselli, *Tell Me How It Ends* (Minneapolis: Coffee House Press, 2017), 25-26.

[3]Luiselli, *Tell Me How It Ends*, 70-71.

[4]Catherine Shoichet, "In Mexico, Central American Immigrants Under Fire," CNN, July 14, 2012, www.cnn.com/2012/07/14/world/americas/mexico-immigrant-shelter/index.html.

[5]La Bestia is a name given to several trains heading to the United States from Mexico, not just one train.

[6]Luiselli, *Tell Me How It Ends*, 27.

[7]Sonia Nazario, *Enrique's Journey* (New York: Random House, 2007), 104.

[8]Nazario, *Enrique's Journey*, 107.

[9]The English translation of this word, *wetback*, is often seen as offensive: "The English term, originally coined after Mexicans illegally entered the U.S. by swimming or wading across the Rio Grande, evolved to include a broader group of immigrants who entered into the country on foot or in cars. The Spanish translation *espaldas mojadas*, is typically shortened to just *mojado* or *mojada*, depending on the person's gender. . . . In 1954, as the U.S. economy sputtered to find its footing after the Korean War, the government launched the now-infamous Operation Wetback, a deportation drive that sent Mexicans back to Mexico in droves and roused complaints of racial profiling and fractured families," Marisa Gerber, "For Latinos, a Spanish Word Loaded with Meaning," *Los Angeles Times*, April 1, 2013, www.latimes.com/local/la-xpm-2013-apr-01-la-me-latino-labels-20130402-story.html.

[10]Gena Thomas, *A Smoldering Wick* (Concord, NC: Self-published, 2017), 72.

[11]Thomas, *A Smoldering Wick*.

[12]US Embassy and Consulates in Mexico, "Adoptions," accessed July 16, 2018, mx.usembassy.gov/visas/adoptions/.

[13]"Understanding the Hague Convention," US Department of State, accessed July 16, 2018, travel.state.gov/content/travel/en/Intercountry-Adoption/Adoption-Process/understanding-the-hague-convention.html.

[14]Becca McBride, *The Globalization of Adoption: Individuals, States, and Agencies Across Borders* (Cambridge: Cambridge University Press, 2016), 95.

[15]Jayakumar Christian, *God of the Empty-Handed* (Monrovia, CA: MARC, 1999), 123.

[16]Christian, *God of the Empty-Handed*.

[17]Ryan Kuja, *From the Inside Out: Reimagining Mission, Recreating the World* (Eugene, OR: Cascade Books, 2018), 58.

5: UNACCOMPANIED MINOR

[1]These numbers were calculated in calendar years through the statistics offered by US Customs and Border Protection, "Southwest Border Migration," www.cbp.gov/newsroom/stats/sw-border-migration.

[2]US Customs, "Southwest Border Migration."

[3]Caitlin Dickerson, "Hundreds of Immigrant Children Have Been Taken from Parents at US Border," *New York Times*, April 20, 2018, www.nytimes .com/2018/04/20/us/immigrant-children-separation-ice.html.

[4]Cleveland Clinic, "Dissociative Amnesia," updated 2018, my.clevelandclinic .org/health/diseases/9789-dissociative-amnesia.

[5]Dylan Gee, "I Study Kids Who Were Separated from Their Parents: The Trauma Could Change Their Brains Forever," Vox, June 20, 2018, www.vox .com/first-person/2018/6/20/17482698/tender-age-family-separation -border-immigrants-children.

[6]Nick Miroff, "Migrants Say U.S. Border Patrol Detention Centers Are 'Iceboxes,'" *Chicago Tribune*, August 7, 2018, www.chicagotribune.com/news /nationworld/ct-migrants-detention-centers-iceboxes-20180807-story.html.

[7]I do not use the word *aliens* to refer to immigrants. It's important to note that this is how the government labels them.

[8]It could be that, like many others who have traveled in the cargo section of semi-trailers, Carlos suffered what a San Antonio fire chief calls "irreversible brain damage." See Holly Yan and Jason Morris, "San Antonio Driver Says He Didn't Know Immigrants Were in Truck," CNN, July 25, 2017, www .cnn.com/2017/07/24/us/san-antonio-trailer-migrants/index.html.

[9]Based on a facility tour taken in August 2018 by the author.

[10]Jacob Saboroff and Julia Ainsley, "McAllen, Texas, Immigration Processing Center Is Largest in US," *NBC News*, June 18, 2018, www.nbcnews.com/news /us-news/mcallen-texas-immigration-processing-center-largest-u-s-n884126.

[11]US Customs and Border Protection, "Immigration Inspection Program," modified February 21, 2014, www.cbp.gov/border-security/ports-entry/overview.

[12]Sara Wise and George Petras, "The Process of Deportation," *USA Today*, June 25, 2018, www.usatoday.com/pages/interactives/graphics/deportation -explainer/.

[13]Dylan Williams Law, "Expedited Removal: How Does the Process Work at the US Port of Entry and What Are the Main Concerns?" October 31, 2016, dyanwilliamslaw.com/2016/10/expedited-removal-how-does-the-process -work-at-the-u-s-port-of-entry/.

[14]American Immigration Council, "A Primer on Expedited Removal," February 3, 2017, www.americanimmigrationcouncil.org/research/primer -expedited-removal.

[15]American Immigration Council, "A Primer."

[16]American Immigration Council, "A Primer."

[17]American Immigration Council, "A Primer."

[18]Caitlin Dickerson, "Hundreds of Immigrant Children Have Been Taken from Parents at US Border," *New York Times*, April 20, 2018, www.nytimes .com/2018/04/20/us/immigrant-children-separation-ice.html.

[19]For more information on this, see Jessica Jones et al., "Betraying Family Values: How Immigration Policy at the United States Border Is Separating Families," Lutheran Immigration and Refugee Service, January 10, 2017, supportkind.org/resources/betraying-family-values/.

[20]Tal Kopan, "New DHS Policy Could Separate Families Caught Crossing the Border Illegally," CNN, May 7, 2018, www.cnn.com/2018/05/07/politics /illegal-immigration-border-prosecutions-families-separated/index.html.

[21]United States Department of Justice, "Attorney General Announces Zero-Tolerance Policy for Criminal Illegal Entry," April 6, 2018, www.justice.gov/opa /pr/attorney-general-announces-zero-tolerance-policy-criminal-illegal-entry.

[22]Sonia Nazario, *Enrique's Journey* (New York: Random House, 2014), 185-86.

[23]Muzaffar Chishti and Faye Hipsman, "Dramatic Surge in the Arrival of Unaccompanied Children Has Deep Roots and No Simple Solution," *Migration Policy Institute*, June 13, 2014, www.migrationpolicy.org/article /dramatic-surge-arrival-unaccompanied-children-has-deep-roots-and-no -simple-solutions.

[24]J. Weston Phippen, "Young, Illegal, and Alone," *Atlantic*, October 15, 2015, www.theatlantic.com/politics/archive/2015/10/unaccompanied-minors -immigrants/410404/.

[25]Office of Refugee Resettlement, "Sponsors and Placement," modified June 30, 2017, www.acf.hhs.gov/orr/about/ucs/sponsors.

[26]Office of Refugee Resettlement, "Sponsors and Placement."

[27]Elise Foley and Roque Planas, "Trump's Crackdown on Immigrant Parents Puts More Kids in an Already Strained System," *Huffington Post*, May 25, 2018, www.huffingtonpost.com/entry/immigrant-children-separated-from -parents_us_5b087b90e4b0802d69cb4070.

[28]Ephrat Livni, "The Problem with the Narrative About 1,500 Children 'Lost' by US Immigration Authorities," *Quartz*, May 28, 2018, qz.com/1290662

/1500-children-were-lost-by-us-immigration-authorities-but-theres-a
-problem-with-that-narrative/.

[29]Eli Hager, "Young Migrants: Victims of Gangs or Members of Them?" *New York Times,* May 1, 2018, www.nytimes.com/2018/05/01/us/immigration
-minors-children.html.

[30]This conversation is based on Julia's first-person account and Jessica's first-person account.

6: DEPENDENT CHILDREN

[1]Rhonda M. Roorda's *In Their Voices: Black Americans on Transracial Adoption* (New York: Columbia University Press, 2015) is not specific to international adoptions but gives a good framework around the complexities of transracial adoption.

[2]Tammy Perlmutter, "5 Dos and Don'ts of Foster Parenting," *Mudroom Blog,* 2018, mudroomblog.com/5-dos-donts-foster-parenting/.

[3]Soong-Chan Rah, *Prophetic Lament* (Downers Grove, IL: InterVarsity Press, 2015), 114.

[4]Originally published as a blog post, Gena Thomas, "A Lament to God for Christ the Foster Child," November 17, 2017, www.genathomas.com/blog/a-lament-to-god-for-christ-the-foster-child.

[5]Originally published as a blog post, Gena Thomas, "The Intertwined Kingdoms of Heaven and Hell," *Mudroom Blog,* March 19, 2018, mudroomblog.com/intertwined-kingdoms-heaven-hell/. Content adapted with permission.

7: FOSTER DAUGHTER

[1]Jessica Lahey, "Every Time Foster Kids Move, They Lose Months of Academic Progress," *Atlantic,* February 28, 2014, www.theatlantic.com/education/archive/2014/02/every-time-foster-kids-move-they-lose-months-of-academic-progress/284134/.

[2]Rita I. Morris, "Voices of Foster Youths: Problems and Ideas for Change," *Urologic Nursing,* 27, no. 5 (2007). www.cbuna.org/sites/default/files/download/members/unjarticles/2007/07oct/419.pdf.

[3]Debbie Noble-Carr et al., "Needs and Experiences of Biological Children of Foster Carers: A Scoping Study," Institute of Child Protection Studies, Australian Catholic University, Canberra, Australia, December 2014, 20, staff.acu.edu.au/__data/assets/pdf_file/0015/712032/Final_report_-_needs_and_experiences_of_biological_children_of_foster_carers,_a_scoping_study.pdf.

8: "¿QUIÉN ES USTED A MÍ?" ("WHO ARE YOU TO ME?")

[1]Cris Beam, *To the End of June* (Boston: Mariner Books, 2013), 76.

[2]Kathy Khang, *Raise Your Voice* (Downers Grove, IL: InterVarsity Press, 2018), 42.

[3]Louise Stewart and Peter Leggat, "Culture Shock and Travelers," *Journal of Travel Medicine* 5, no. 2 (1998): 84-88.

[4]Laila Lalami, "What Does It Take to 'Assimilate in America,'" *New York Times Magazine*, August 1, 2017, www.nytimes.com/2017/08/01/magazine/what -does-it-take-to-assimilate-in-america.html.

[5]M. Daniel Caroll R., *Christians at the Border: Immigration, the Church, and the Bible* (Grand Rapids: Brazos Press, 2013), 78.

[6]Doug Stanglin, "Immigrant Children: Federal Judge Orders Families Separated at Border Be Reunited Within 30 Days," *USA Today*, June 27, 2018, www.usatoday.com/story/news/politics/2018/06/27/judge-orders-families -separated-border-reunited-within-30-days/737194002/.

9: REUNIFICATION/*REUNIFICACIÓN*

[1]Nick Miroff, "A Family Was Separated at the Border, and This Distraught Father Took His Own Life," *Washington Post*, June 9, 2018, www.washington post.com/world/national-security/a-family-was-separated-at-the-border -and-this-distraught-father-took-his-own-life/2018/06/08/24e40b70-6b5d -11e8-9e38-24e693b38637_story.html?utm_term=.6e8cf0bbf8b7.

[2]International Society for Traumatic Stress Studies, "Recovered Memories of Childhood Trauma," accessed July 9, 2018, www.istss.org/public-resources /remembering-childhood-trauma.aspx.

10: REFLECTIONS

[1]Robert Stribley, "The Way We Speak About Unauthorized Immigrants Matters," *Huffington Post*, September 6, 2017, www.huffingtonpost.com/entry /the-language-of-illegal-immigration_us_58076b62e4b00483d3b5cdba.

[2]Ursula Kenny, "Francisco Cantú: 'This Is Work That Endangers the Soul,'" *Guardian*, February 18, 2018, www.theguardian.com/books/2018/feb/18 /francisco-cantu-line-becomes-river-interview-former-us-border-patrol-agent.

[3]Jose Antonio Vargas, "Immigration Debate: The Problem with the Word *Illegal*," *Time*, September 21, 2017, ideas.time.com/2012/09/21/immigration -debate-the-problem-with-the-word-illegal/.

[4]Vargas, "Immigration Debate."

[5]Centro de Derechos de Mujeres, *Voces, Silencios y Cicatrices de La Violencia Contra Las Mujeres: Relatos de Vida de Mujeres Defensoras*, 10.

[6]Centro de Derechos de Mujeres, *Voces*, 7.

[7]Centro de Derechos de Mujeres, *Voces*, 5.

[8]Rosa Martha Zárate, "Lucha, Poder, Esperanza," in Ada María Isasi-Díaz, *Mujerista Theology* (Maryknoll, NY: Orbis, 1996), 180-81.

[9]Isasi-Díaz, *Mujerista Theology*, 65.

[10]Valeria Luiselli, *Tell Me How It Ends* (Minneapolis: Coffee House Press, 2017), 46.

[11] Luiselli, *Tell Me*, 24.

[12]Kenny, "Francisco Cantú."

[13]Craig Stewart, "Rainbows Tattooed Over Open Wounds," Medium, medium .com/@craigdstewart/rainbows-tattooed-over-open-wounds-5fc06940763.

[14]Soong-Chan Rah, *Prophetic Lament* (Downers Grove, IL: InterVarsity Press, 2015), 51.

[15]Rah, *Prophetic Lament*, 67.

[16]Published as "A Lament to God for Christ the Immigrant," Missio Alliance, September 7, 2017, www.missioalliance.org/immigrant-lament/.

[17]Interview with Pastor Gricel Medina, April 17, 2018, for my personal blog, www.genathomas.com/blog/interview-with-pastor-gricel-medina.

[18]This and the three following indented quotes are from personal communication with Adam Estle, August 31, 2018.

[19]LifeWay Research, "Evangelical Views on Immigration," February 2015, lifewayresearch.com/wp-content/uploads/2015/03/Evangelical-Views-on -Immigration-Report.pdf.

[20]If you're interested in fostering an unaccompanied minor, check with your local Catholic Charities office to find out more about local foster-care needs. For more information specifically about fostering an unaccompanied minor, go to the United States Conference of Catholic Bishops' webpage, www.usccb .org/about/children-and-migration/foster-care/index.cfm, or Lutheran Immigration and Refugee Services, www.lirs.org/foster-care-programs-partners/. Both agencies work directly with the Office of Refugee Resettlement.

[21]Matthew Soerens and Jenny Yang, *Welcoming the Stranger* (Downers Grove, IL: InterVarsity Press, 2018), 236.

[22]Jonathan Merritt, "Lauren Daigle and the Lost Art of Discernment," *Atlantic*, December 8, 2018, www.theatlantic.com/ideas/archive/2018/12 /let-lauren-daigle-be-unsure-about-lgbt-relationships/577651/.

[23]Lauren Pearle, "Trump Administration Unsure if Thousands More Migrant Families Were Separated Than Originally Estimated, Legal Filing Shows," ABC News, February 2, 2019, abcnews.go.com/beta-story-container/US /trump-administration-unsure-thousands-migrant-families-separated -originally/story?id=60797633.

[24]Michael Wear, "Rising Above Partisanship," Q Ideas.org, YouTube, 2018, www.youtube.com/watch?v=ZnF4mkh3Vmc.

[25]In her book *Disunity in Christ*, Christena Cleveland talks about how we all have perceptions of who we think is the wrong type of Christian and the right type of Christian. She calls them Right Christian and Wrong Christian.

APPENDIX A

[1]A few books on culture shock and assimilation: *The Poisonwood Bible* by Barbara Kingsolver; *When They Call You a Terrorist* by Patrisse Khan-Cullors and Asha Bandele; *From the Inside Out* by Ryan Kuja; *Lucky Boy* by Shanthi Sekaran; and *Assimilate or Go Home* by D. L. Mayfield.

APPENDIX B

[1]Guillermo Anderson, "Cipota de Barrio," copyright © 2001 Costa Norte Records.

GLOSSARY

ACF—Administration for Children and Families is a division of the Department of Health and Human Services that, according to its website, promotes economic and social well-being of children and families.

Coyote—The term used to describe smugglers or guides that are paid to bring people across the US-Mexico border.

DHHS—Department of Health and Human Services, which houses social services departments. One of the fifteen executive departments, DHHS is the umbrella department for Administration for Children and Families (ACF), Administration for Community Living (ACL), Agency for Healthcare Research and Quality (AHRQ), Agency for Toxic Substances and Disease Registry (ATSDR), Center for Faith-Based and Neighborhood Partnerships (CFBNP), Centers for Disease Control and Prevention (CDC), Centers for Medicare and Medicaid Services (CMS), Departmental Appeals Board (DAB), Food and Drug Administration (FDA), Health Resources and Services Administration (HRSA), Indian Health Service (IHS), National Institutes of Health (NIH), Office for Civil Rights (OCR), Office of Global Affairs (OGA), Office of Inspector General (OIG), Office of Intergovernmental and External Affairs (IEA), Office of Medicare Hearings and Appeals (OMHA), Office of the Chief Technology Officer (CTO), Office of the General Counsel (OGC), Office of the National Coordinator for Health Information Technology (ONC), Substance Abuse and Mental Health Services Administration (SAMHSA), among many assistant secretaries' offices.

DHS—Department of Homeland Security. One of the fifteen executive departments, DHS is the umbrella department for US Citizenship and Immigration Services (USCIS), US Customs and Border Protection

(CBP), US Coast Guard (USCG), Federal Management Agency (FEMA), Federal Law Enforcement Training Center (FLETC), US Immigration and Customs Enforcement (ICE), Transportation Security Administration (TSA), US Secret Service (USSS), Management Directorate, National Protection and Programs Directorate, Science and Technology Directorate, Countering Weapons of Mass Destruction Office, Office of Intelligence and Analysis, and Office of Operations Coordination.

ICE—Immigrations and Customs Enforcement is a law enforcement agency created in 2003 under the Department of Homeland Security. It enforces laws governing border control, customs, trade, and immigration. This agency was created as a merger between two former agencies: US Customs Service and the Immigration and Naturalization Service. According to its website, ICE's annual budget is $6 billion, which covers Homeland Security Investigations (HSI), Enforcement and Removal Operations (ERO), Office of the Principal Legal Advisor (OPLA), and Management and Administration.

ORR—Office of Refugee Resettlement is under the Administration for Children and Families (ACF) of the Department of Health and Human Services.

Smuggled—An adjective used to describe someone who paid a smuggler, otherwise known as a coyote, to bring him or her across the border.

Trafficked—An adjective used to describe someone who was brought across the border by force, fraud, or coercion.

TVPRA—William Wilberforce Trafficking Victims Protection Reauthorization Act of 2008, which aims to prevent people from becoming victims of human trafficking.

UAC—Unaccompanied alien child, a title given to children who are under the age of eighteen, were not authorized to enter the United States, and are without a parent or legal guardian. Note that this may include children who cross into the United States with a grandparent, aunt, or other caregiver, but then are separated by the government.

RECOMMENDED READING

BIBLICAL JUSTICE AND MISSION

Christian, Jayakumar. *God of the Empty-Handed*. Monrovia, CA: MARC, 1999.

Khang, Kathy. *Raise Your Voice: Why We Stay Silent and How to Speak Up*. Downers Grove, IL: InterVarsity Press, 2018.

Kuja, Ryan. *From the Inside Out: Reimagining Mission, Recreating the World*. Eugene, OR: Cascade Books, 2018.

Rah, Soong-Chan. *Prophetic Lament: A Call for Justice in Troubled Times*. Downers Grove, IL: InterVarsity Press, 2015.

Thomas, Gena. *A Smoldering Wick: Igniting Missions Work with Sustainable Practices*. Concord, NC: Self Published, 2017.

Warren, Michelle. *The Power of Proximity: Moving Beyond Awareness to Action*. Downers Grove, IL: InterVarsity Press, 2017.

CHRISTIANS AND IMMIGRATION

Carroll R., M. Daniel. *Christians at the Border: Immigration, the Church, and the Bible*. Grand Rapids: Brazos Press, 2013.

LifeWay Research. "Evangelical Views on Immigration." February 2015. http://lifewayresearch.com/wp-content/uploads/2015/03/Evangelical-Views-on-Immigration-Report.pdf.

Soerens, Matthew and Jenny Yang. *Welcoming the Stranger: Justice, Compassion, and Truth in the Immigration Debate*. Downers Grove, IL: InterVarsity Press, 2018.

CULTURE SHOCK AND ASSIMILATION

Kingsolver, Barbara. *The Poisonwood Bible*. New York: Harper Collins, 1998.

Lalami, Laila. "What Does It Take to 'Assimilate' in America?" *The New York Times Magazine*, August 1, 2017. www.nytimes.com/2017/08/01 /magazine/what-does-it-take-to-assimilate-in-america.html.

Mayfield, D. L. *Assimilate or Go Home: Notes from a Failed Missionary on Rediscovering Faith.* New York: HarperOne, 2016.

Stewart, Louise and Peter A. Leggat. "Culture Shock and Travelers." *Journal of Travel Medicine* 5, no. 2 (1998): 84-88. www.ncbi.nlm.nih .gov/pubmed/9772322.

CROSSING THE BORDER

Cantú, Francisco. *The Line Becomes a River.* New York: Riverhead Books, 2018.

Hallock, Jeffrey, Ariel G. Ruiz Soto, and Michael Fix. *In Search of Safety, Growing Numbers of Women Flee Central America.* Migration Policy Institute, May 30, 2018. www.migrationpolicy.org/article/search-safety -growing-numbers-women-flee-central-america.

Nazario, Sonia. *Enrique's Journey.* New York: Random House, 2014.

Shetty, Salil. "Most Dangerous Journey: What Central American Migrants Face When They Try to Cross the Border." *Amnesty International.* Accessed July 10, 2018. www.amnestyusa.org/most-dangerous -journey-what-central-american-migrants-face-when-they-try-to -cross-the-border/.

DEPORTATION AND IMMIGRATION POLICY

American Immigration Council. "A Primer on Expedited Removal." February 3, 2017. www.americanimmigrationcouncil.org/research/primer -expedited-removal.

Jones, Jessica, Katharina Obser, and Jennifer Podkul. "Betraying Family Values: How Immigration Policy at the United States Border is Separating Families." KIND, January 10, 2017. https://supportkind.org /resources/betraying-family-values/.

Tory, Sarah and Paige Blankenbuehler. "How Private Prisons Became a Booming Business." *The Journal*, May 16, 2017. https://the-journal .com/articles/47607.

Wise, Sara and George Petras. "The Process of Deportation." *USA Today*, June 25,2018. www.usatoday.com/pages/interactives/graphics /deportation-explainer/.

FOSTER CARE AND FOSTERING REFUGEES

Beam, Cris. *Till the End of June: The Intimate Life of American Foster Care.* Boston: Mariner Books, 2013.

Bethany Christian Services. "Refugee Children in Crisis." https://bethany .org/help-a-child/foster-care/refugee-foster-care.

Morris, R. "Voices of Foster Youths: Problems and Ideas for Change." *Urologic Nursing* 27, no. 5 (2007). Retrieved from www.cbuna.org/sites /default/files/download/members/unjarticles/2007/07oct/419.pdf.

Office of Refugee Resettlement. "Sponsors and Placement." Last modified June 30, 2017. www.acf.hhs.gov/orr/about/ucs/sponsors.

Perlmutter, Tammy. "5 Dos and Don'ts of Foster Parenting." Mudroom Blog, 2018. http://mudroomblog.com/5-dos-donts-foster-parenting/.

Rhodes-Courter, Ashley. *Three Little Words: A Memoir.* New York: Atheneum, 2008.

Sckaran, Shanthi. *Lucky Boy.* New York: G. P. Putnam's Sons, 2016.

United States Conference of Catholic Bishops. "Foster Care for Unaccompanied Children." www.usccb.org/about/children-and-migration /unaccompanied-refugee-minor-program/index.cfm.

TRAUMA

Gee, Dylan. "I Study Kids Who Were Separated from Their Parents. The Trauma Could Change Their Brains Forever." Vox, June 20, 2018. www .vox.com/first-person/2018/6/20/17482698/tender-age-family-separation -border-immigrants-children.

International Society for Traumatic Stress Studies. "Adult Survivors of Childhood Trauma and Recovered Memories." Accessed July 9, 2018. www.istss.org/public-resources/remembering-childhood-trauma.aspx.

Van der Kolk, Bessel A. *The Body Keeps the Score: Brain, Mind, and Body in the Healing of Trauma.* New York: Penguin Books, 2015.

UNACCOMPANIED MINORS

Chishti, Muzaffar and Faye Hipsman. "Dramatic Surge in the Arrival of Unaccompanied Children Has Deep Roots and No Simple Solution." June 13, 2014: Migration Policy Institute: www.migrationpolicy.org /article/dramatic-surge-arrival-unaccompanied-children-has-deep -roots-and-no-simple-solutions.

Luiselli, Valeria. *Tell Me How It Ends: An Essay in Forty Questions.* Minneapolis: Coffee House Press, 2017.

Phippen, J. Weston. "Young, Illegal, and Alone." *Atlantic,* October 15, 2015. www.theatlantic.com/politics/archive/2015/10/unaccompanied-minors -immigrants/410404/.

WOMEN'S RIGHTS AND ENVIRONMENTALISM

Centro de Derechos de Mujeres. *Voces, Silencios y Cicatrices de La Violencia Contra Las Mujeres: Relatos de Vida de Mujeres Defensoras.* Tegucigalpa, Honduras: Comunica, 2017.

Chircop, Andrea. "An Ecofeminist Conceptual Framework to Explore Gendered Environmental Health Inequities in Urban Dettings and to Inform Healthy Public Policy." *Nursing Inquiry* 15, no. 2 (2008): 135-47. www.ncbi.nlm.nih.gov/pubmed/18476856.

Isai-Díaz, Ada. *Mujerista Theology.* Maryknoll, NY: Orbis Books, 1996.

ZERO-TOLERANCE POLICY

Dickerson, Caitlin. "Hundreds of Immigrant Children Have Been Taken from Parents at U.S. Border." *New York Times,* April 20, 2018. www .nytimes.com/2018/04/20/us/immigrant-children-separation-ice.html.

Gonzales, Richard. "Trump's Executive Order on Family Separation: What It Does and Doesn't Do." NPR, June 20, 2018. www.npr.org /2018/06/20/622095441/trump-executive-order-on-family-separation -what-it-does-and-doesnt-do.

Hager, Eli. "Young Migrants: Victims of Gangs or Members of Them?" *New York Times,* May 1, 2018. www.nytimes.com/2018/05/01/us /immigration-minors-children.html.

Pearle, Lauren. "Trump Administration Unsure If Thousands More Migrant Families Were Separated Than Originally Estimated, Legal Filing Shows." ABC News, February 2, 2019. https://abcnews.go.com/beta-story-container/US/trump-administration-unsure-thousands-migrant-families-separated-originally/story?id=60797633.

United States Department of Justice. "Attorney General Announces Zero-Tolerance Policy for Criminal Illegal Entry." April 6, 2018. www.justice.gov/opa/pr/attorney-general-announces-zero-tolerance-policy-criminal-illegal-entry.

ABOUT THE AUTHOR

Gena Thomas is a writer, author, and speaker. She and Andrew have been married for over a decade. They have two children.

From 2009 to 2013, Andrew and Gena were missionaries in northern Mexico, where they started a coffee-shop ministry, El Búho (The Owl). The shop still serves the local and international population near Potrero Chico, a climbing hot spot outside Monterrey. During their time in Mexico, Gena began her graduate studies in International Development through Eastern University. She graduated with her master's in 2014. She now works as an instructional designer at a nonprofit that empowers others through holistic development.

Gena has written for several Christian publications, including *Christianity Today* and *Missio Alliance*. She published her first book, *A Smoldering Wick: Igniting Missions Work with Sustainable Practices*, in 2017.

Gena would be happy to connect with you on Twitter @genaLthomas.